Don't Forget About the Adjuncts!

A volume in
Research, Theory, and Practice Within Academic Affairs
Antione D. Tomlin and Sherella Cupid, *Series Editors*

Don't Forget About the Adjuncts!

edited by

Antione D. Tomlin
Anne Arundel Community College

INFORMATION AGE PUBLISHING, INC.
Charlotte, NC • www.infoagepub.com

Library of Congress Cataloging-in-Publication Data

A CIP record for this book is available from the Library of Congress
http://www.loc.gov

ISBN: 979-8-88730-236-2 (Paperback)
979-8-88730-237-9 (Hardcover)
979-8-88730-238-6 (E-Book)

Copyright © 2023 Information Age Publishing Inc.

All rights reserved. No part of this publication may be reproduced, stored in a
retrieval system, or transmitted, in any form or by any means, electronic, mechanical,
photocopying, microfilming, recording or otherwise, without written permission
from the publisher.

Printed in the United States of America

CONTENTS

Introduction... vii
Antione D. Tomlin

PART I
MY EXPERIENCE MATTERS

1 Working as an Adjunct With DisABILITY............................ 3
L. Denise Portis

2 What They Won't Tell You: Dos and Don'ts to Adjuncting
While in the Academe.. 13
Leslie Ekpe, Ashlee Daniels, and Sylviane Greensword

3 Prioritizing Adjuncts: Revisiting the Impact of Part-Time
Educators, Leaders, and Entrepreneurs............................... 27
Sierra JêCre McKissick

4 Both Sides of the Fence.. 43
Danny E. Malone, Jr.

PART II

THE VALUE OF CONTINUOUS IMPROVEMENT

5 Improving the Instructional Skills of Adjunct Faculty Through Professional Development 51
Ramycia McGhee

6 To Be an African Centered Educator in 21st Century Social Work Education 63
Senemeht Olatunji

7 Ten Commandments for Adjuncts 73
Erica Heflin-Queen

8 What Adjunct Faculty Need to Be Successful in the *Online* Classroom? 81
Lealan M. Zaccone and Sandra C. Hannigan

9 The Invisible Educator: Are Adjunct Teachers Undervalued? 95
Raleta S. Dawkins, Sabrina Hinton, and Saleena Frazier

PART III

I TEACH BECAUSE I LOVE IT, NOT TO PAY THE BILLS

10 Through the Lens of a "Have-Not": An Adjunct Faculty's View 107
Karen Marie Wagner-Clarke

11 The Unsung Hero 119
Loubert Senatus

12 Life on the Bubble 125
Shelagh Smith

About the Editor 133

About the Contributors 135

INTRODUCTION

Working as an adjunct can be rewarding and frustrating at the same time. With low pay, unpredictable class cuts, and lack of autonomy in many cases, adjuncts could find themselves questioning their why. That is their reason for saying yes each semester. Adjunct is difficult and thankless work. We must not forget the adjuncts, as I genuinely believe they are the backbone of most higher education institutions.

Adjuncts, their work, and their commitment to higher education and students mean the world to me, as I was an adjunct for 5 years before becoming full-time faculty. I do recognize that not all adjuncts strive to be full-time faculty. So, this text will explore multiple perspectives, paths, and career trajectories of adjunct faculty. My experience as adjunct faculty, while rewarding, was a bit frustrating. So, my hope with this book is that we remember the adjuncts and just how much sacrifice they make to support institutional and student success. So, thank you to all adjuncts, as your work and expertise are crucial to all higher education institutions.

One of this book's aims is to allow adjuncts to share their experiences navigating workspaces as frequently undervalued faculty in higher education. Adjuncts often work with less while still being expected to perform in many ways, like a full-time faculty member. From promotions to classroom evaluations and professional development, many adjuncts are held to the same standards as full-time faculty. This text will share some of the ins and outs, opportunities and challenges, and joys and frustrations adjunct faculty experience as part-time faculty. This book highlights the adjunct faculty voice, as it is a text by adjuncts for adjuncts. The 17 contributing authors in this

---

Don't Forget About the Adjuncts!, pages vii–ix
Copyright © 2023 by Information Age Publishing
www.infoagepub.com
All rights of reproduction in any form reserved.

viii ▪ Introduction

text share their stories for the betterment of themselves, their students, and higher education as a whole. Together, they provide more insight into understanding the experiences of adjunct faculty in higher education institutions.

While each chapter's stories, lessons, wisdom, and advice differ, each chapter follows a similar structure. Each author shares their lived experiences while sharing some about their adjunct role and expertise. Next, the chapters explore challenges and opportunities experienced. Then tips, strategies, and advice for potential and current adjunct faculty are provided, along with global recommendations for administration and higher education institutions. Last, each chapter ends with words of affirmation to help support their journey as adjuncts. We include these affirmations in hopes that they will add to the support and encourage adjuncts to make decisions that allow them to practice self-care and make decisions that will aid in their success.

This book explores three parts crafted organically from the opportunities, challenges, advice, and recommendations the authors share in their chapters. The parts used as a foundation for sharing the stories of this text include (a) "My Experience Matters," (b) "The Value of Continuous Improvement," and (c) "I Teach Because I Love It, Not to Pay the Bills." As mentioned previously, each chapter follows a specific flow and organization. The parts listed serve as a background to a larger conversation that the text is generally entering about the experiences of adjunct faculty. Below, more details of each part are described.

PART 1: MY EXPERIENCE MATTERS

This part explores the expertise and knowledge that adjunct faculty bring to the educational environment. Within this part, adjunct faculty talk about feeling less than full-time faculty in many ways. This part also speaks to the different intersections and identities that adjunct faculty bring to their role, that sometimes are not valued and/or respected. Additionally, contributing authors in this section speak to all they bring to the institution and students and the assets they are because of their dynamic wealth and expertise, and knowledge, which all too often go unacknowledged.

PART 2: THE VALUE OF CONTINUOUS IMPROVEMENT

This part delved into professional development and how adjuncts continue to master and hone their skills in the profession. For promotion to a higher adjunct status, to gain full-time employment, or to demonstrate commitment to continuing securing classes for future semesters, the adjuncts in this section made it clear that professional development was of the utmost importance. It was clear that to continue being successful as an adjunct, continuing to learn and grow is necessary for self and long-term career success. Leaning into the idea of continuous improvement was something these adjuncts felt was pivotal to maintaining their active adjunct status or potentially transitioning to full-time faculty.

PART 3: I TEACH BECAUSE I LOVE IT, NOT TO PAY THE BILLS

Often when we think of adjuncts, what comes to mind is overworked and underpaid. While this is the case, most times, the adjuncts who work because it is extra income or for other motivations outside of paying the bills are sometimes overlooked. This section explores the experiences of adjuncts who do not need the income to have basic needs met or who know that they are not going to become rich from adjuncting. These adjuncts focus more on their passion for teaching and explicitly share that they know adjuncting was never a means of primary income.

We, as a team, know we have a responsibility to be sure that readers know that the stories you will read and learn from do not represent all adjunct experiences. So, we encourage you to take each story as an individual scene that adds to a film. Each chapter helps to tell the story, but in no way is this the entire story. We further encourage you to explore any reactions, emotions, or feelings that may arise from diving into all that these adjuncts have to say.

In true tradition, I end this chapter by saying thank you to the 17 contributing authors. They have committed their experiences, hard work, and stories to further the conversation on what it means to be an adjunct in higher education. To L. Denise, Leslie, Ashlee, Sylviane, Sierra, Danny, Ramycia, Senemeht, Erica, Lealan, Sandy, Raleta, Sabrina, Saleena, Karen, Loubert, and Shelagh, thank you! All of your hard work, dedication, and commitment to your profession is what makes higher education institutions so special. Please, continue being great and bringing your expertise to your students.

— Antione D. Tomlin

PART I

MY EXPERIENCE MATTERS

CHAPTER 1

WORKING AS AN ADJUNCT WITH DISABILITY

L. Denise Portis

ABSTRACT

The number of individuals with a disability and over the age of 18 in the United States includes 26% (1 in 4) of the population (Centers for Disease Control and Prevention, 2020). Recent statistics report that there are over 260,000 adjuncts working in the United States (Zippia, 2022), with as many as 67,600 of those adjuncts having some form of visible or invisible disability. Adjuncts with disabilities have a unique opportunity to help raise awareness on their campuses. Adjuncts with disabilities may influence diversity, equity, inclusion, and accessibility (DEIA) procedures and generally are welcomed voices on committees tasked with managing and implementing best practices. Employee Resource Groups comprised of adjuncts with disabilities may play an integral role in changing attitudes and environments that will ultimately benefit everyone. Disability for most is a challenge, yet many adjuncts with disabilities have managed to use these challenges to provide measurable examples of posttraumatic growth (PTG). PTG is described as any positive change resulting from the experience of a significant life crisis or traumatic event (Tedeschi et al., 2018). These examples benefit students with disability and encourage them to make a difference in their own future workplaces.

Don't Forget About the Adjuncts!, pages 3–11
Copyright © 2023 by Information Age Publishing
www.infoagepub.com
All rights of reproduction in any form reserved.

4 ▪ L. D. PORTIS

I have been teaching for 22 years, 11 years as an adjunct professor of psychology and American Sign Language at Maryland community colleges. As a child I suffered a traumatic brain injury. Subsequent surgeries and complications produced profound hearing loss and significant mobility challenges by the time I was 25 years old. It took me 16 years to finish college and earn the PhD I so desired. In the years I was in school, however, I began a journey of advocacy and education for those who live with an acquired disability. I traveled extensively providing workshops and seminars on hearing loss, disability challenges in relationships, coping skills, service dogs, posttraumatic growth (PTG), and living with a disability. I was appointed by County Executive Steven Schuh to serve on Anne Arundel County's Commission on Disability Issues (CODI) as vice-chair in 2017 and reappointed by County Executive Steuart Pittman in 2020 as chair. In this role, I have continued to share experiences as a working adjunct with disabilities. I have helped to train college campus security departments, Anne Arundel County first responders, law enforcement, and fire department personnel in serving and protecting people with disabilities. I continue to work with CODI members to plan, promote, and execute the county's Disability Awareness Day each October. I currently teach as an adjunct professor at two Maryland community colleges. In 2019, I was recognized by the League for Innovation with the John & Suanne Roueche Excellence Award. In 2021, Anne Arundel Community College nominated me with the Equity & Inclusion Champion Award in recognition of the "disABILITY for a Day" assignment required in my courses and for my ongoing campus and community advocacy efforts. I actively participate in campus committees to promote accessibility and inclusion and advise student clubs, modeling an example and encouraging students to do the same. I am currently matched with my third service dog, Finn (a golden retriever), and he accompanies me to all classes and campus events. You may read some of our adventures and other essays on disability at my 25-year-old blog, "Hearing Elmo."

CHALLENGES FOR AN ADJUNCT WITH A DISABILITY

In discussions with other adjuncts with disabilities, I believe the first challenge is to decide whether to disclose the disability. This decision is very personal. There may be circumstances and environments that disclosing a disability is unnecessary. If a disability is invisible, one may choose to navigate as a faculty member without disclosure. Having navigated teaching environments in both high schools and community colleges, I have discovered that disclosure is an important first step. I may have chosen differently if my lifelong vocation was anything other than education. Although my disabilities are very visible now because I have a bedazzled cochlear implant, cane, and use a service dog, my disabilities could fly under the radar and be invisible if I really wanted them to be. However, I determined that for me, it was important to teach by example and therefore, disclosed as early as interviewing for the positions to teach at local colleges. I wanted my students to know that a person with a disability was simply differently abled and could work and thrive. It may not be necessary to disclose a disability during the hiring process, but a person with a disability will need to disclose to access reasonable accommodations under the protection of the Americans With Disabilities Act (ADA) and Rehabilitation Act. The U.S. Department of Labor (n.d.) reports that "an employer is only required to provide work-related accommodations if you disclose your disability to the appropriate individuals" (para. 2). As a person who has lived with a disability for nearly 3 decades, I have discovered disclosure is important as I do need and rely on various workplace accommodations through human resources and various department supervisors. As an adjunct professor, I have also discovered how important transparency is to my students. Emerging evidence in research suggests that attitudes about people with disabilities are heavily influenced by contact with and interaction with someone who is transparent about their disability (Bogart et al., 2022). I also have numerous students who have disclosed to the class various disabilities and did so because of my own example. In a Psychology of Women course, the class and I were discussing and learning about self-identity and the intersectionality of "who" we are. I wrote on the board "I AM" and asked students to come up and complete the phrase. Many put adjectives, and descriptive nouns that identified their race, worldview, ethnicity, culture, sexual orientation, beliefs, and skills. As I watched them huddle around the board to write, I noticed that 100% of the class also completed the phrase with various disabilities, challenges, and mental health disorders. I simply was unable to hold back the tears. Students commiserated with me after I explained why I was emotional about this, but they explained that my example had taught them to own every piece of who they are.

Another challenge that an adjunct with a disability faces, is the decision about how to self-identify with the campus community. The American Psychological Association (APA) recognizes that the person with disability may choose person-first language (PFL) or identity-first language (IFL; American Psychological Association, 2020). My own experience has taught me to be more fluid with this decision as at times it is important to be identified as a person first. For example, when my work or voice is expressed as a peer to colleagues, I choose PFL and those around me follow my lead. However, when I am acting as a disability advocate, I prefer IFL as this provides real-life expertise as I participate. I have also discovered my choice of language is often dependent on the environment and circumstances detailing my physical disabilities or mental health disabilities. To avoid perpetuating the stigma often associated with my mental health challenges, depression and panic disorder (Jackson, 2020), I will use PFL. When I am speaking and working as a person with a disability, I use IFL as I may then address specific accommodations and changes needed to provide accessibility to those who need it. Ladau (2021) points out that whether you choose PFL or IFL, omit the word "handicap" whenever possible. It took me a while to stop saying "handicap parking." A more inclusive term is "accessible parking" or "accessible entrance." I realized that the word handicap focused on the negative and did not improve thoughts and assumptions about people with disabilities. Disability should not be equated with something broken. With proper accessibility resources and options, people with a disability can work and thrive in the same environments as abled people. Encouraging the use of "accessible" simply emphasized all that I have pushed for in DEIA guidelines.

OPPORTUNITIES FOR AN ADJUNCT WITH A DISABILITY

There are numerous opportunities for an adjunct with a disability to influence and impact policy and procedures on campus. Many campus barriers are eliminated when adjuncts with a disability serve in various roles, destroying previous social constructs that defined people with a disability as someone with limitations rather than assets (Halder & Assaf, 2017). To be impactful, one must first learn everything you can about the laws that impact people with disability, as well as relational leadership practices. In higher education, a person with a disability will likely find an atmosphere welcoming of personal experience and expertise to train and inform others. Dirth and Branscombe (2018) explain how social identity and personal perspectives may impact DEIA policies and procedures on college campuses, to build efficacy, cohesion, and promote lasting change. One influential platform is that of employee resource groups (ERGs).

In the Spring of 2020 and prior to campus restrictions to the pandemic, my primary employer as an adjunct professor had just begun the process of implementing and activating ERGs. Along with the assistance of a college staff person with an invisible illness, a staff person with a disability, and three faculty members with visible and invisible disabilities, I found the support for launching a disability ERG from human resources, department chairs, deans, and even the president of the college. The ERG I was tagged to co-lead was also given permission to publish an e-newsletter once a month to disseminate to all faculty and staff. March of 2020, changed the timeline for implementing these voluntary, employee-led groups, charged to foster DEIA development on campus. Experts on community college enrollment and completion agree that we are working and living a "new normal" as higher education may never return to what it looked like in early 2020 (Freedberg, 2022). Within this "new normal," I and others in this proposed ERG are starting over in our efforts to launch. This is in part, because of leadership changes and new hires that are DEIA and ADA scripted, but also because the pandemic itself has created a new disability group for those who are immune compromised. *Long COVID-19* is now recognized as a disability under the ADA, Section 504 and 1557 (U.S. Department of Health & Human Services, 2021). With these changes impacting all higher education jobs, I would like to provide some recommendations for both potential adjuncts with disabilities, and for those who are already working as adjuncts.

Recommendations for Adjunct With Disabilities

Before providing several ways adjuncts with disabilities can maximize their effectiveness and influence, I highly recommend implementing these practices with the mindset of a lifelong learner. Like any area of expertise, research in all areas of disabilities is constantly changing. Technology and medical advances continue to change and impact the disability community. As a person with hearing loss and a cochlear implant, I also speech read. Post-pandemic, I am teaching face-to-face again and have discovered that face masks are a communication challenge for me. Immune-compromised or unvaccinated students are wearing masks that hide most of their face and muffle their volume. Early in the pandemic, clear face masks were quickly developed and sold to enable those who speech read the ability to communicate. Because advances like these are ongoing, people with a disability must stay current on technology, medical advances, research, state and federal laws, and DEIA initiatives.

I encourage adjuncts with disabilities to carve out some time each month in advocacy efforts. I have found that county involvement with disability issues is a major source of growth and impact. I started as a volunteer, attending monthly meetings with my local county commission on disability issues. Eventually I was appointed as a voting member and officer. I have found this source of information and advocacy opportunities as a way to stay current on disability laws. I have also been able to educate myself on other disabilities. To be a disability advocate, I knew I had to learn about the challenges others faced, living with disabilities that I do not have. Search your county or city's websites for disability advocacy committees, commissions, and disability workforce agencies.

Colleges offer and often require internal professional development for all college employees including adjuncts. First-person training and workshops on disabilities are often welcome. Volunteering to provide training for the campus community advances DEIA initiatives and also provides a way for your name to be recognized as a person with some expertise in disability issues. Morris (1996) argues that highlighting who you are and how you work and use accommodations on campus, changes how you view yourself. In "Pride Against Prejudice: Transforming Attitudes to Disability," first-person examples of living and working with a disability ultimately and dramatically change how abled people interact with and value people with disabilities (Morris, 1996). Reach out to your campus ADA compliance officer and student disability services departments to request opportunities to train and present cooperatively. To gain disability training experience, contact local senior centers and offer to provide volunteer workshops on disability technology, accommodations, research, coping skills, and local resources and support groups.

I found that being transparent about my disabilities in the classroom, students became more confident about self-disclosure themselves. An atmosphere that welcomes, values, and supports living true-to-self, encouraged both abled students and those with disability to actively seek ways to engage in social justice activities (Jackson, 2020). Disability can easily be integrated in all disciplines. Purposefully seek out current news stories, research and community activities that can be incorporated in class discussions and extra credit activities. Disability is interdisciplinary and can transform the courses you teach to encourage students to make DEIA practices a lifelong habit (Goodley, 2017).

Early in my career in higher education, I looked for ways to mentor students with disabilities. I found that disability student service departments are very welcome to faculty participating in students with disability clubs, activities, and awareness initiatives. I highly recommend volunteering to advise a student club with a disability focus. Participating in this way ultimately allowed the campus culture itself to improve for people with a disability (Halder & Assaf, 2017). I also volunteer as a mentor with the APA. I am matched with one or two graduate students each year and check in with those I am mentoring for 30–60 minutes once a month or more. One does not need to be a member of the APA, so any adjunct with disability can apply. The goal is to promote inclusion and aid in the retention of people with disabilities in psychology's academic programs and careers (APA, n.d.). I have also found that training and networking through the ADA Trainer Leadership Network to be instrumental in gaining community needs assessment training, consulting, and relationship building. This national network has provided valuable support and material to assist in campus and community training. You may find both national and regional associations and training at the ADA National Network (ADATA.org, n.d.).

PERSONAL AFFIRMATIONS THAT PROMOTED GROWTH AND IMPACT

Like many with acquired disabilities, coping with life changes can be a daunting and challenging time. Although I initially struggled and floundered when changes in my abilities occurred, I have found that these challenges also served as the impetus for measurable growth. I became interested in PTG research prior to my dissertation studies. Calhoun and Tedeschi (2014) identified five domains of PTG that include personal strength, new possibilities, relating to other people, appreciation of life, and spiritual change. At first, it took a little bit of work to recognize the positive results of being a person with disabilities. Because of the balance disorder I have, I have had 11 concussions in 9 years. It is easy to focus on the disability and challenges. I do know people with acquired disabilities who have posttraumatic stress disorder (PTSD). This is especially true of veterans with disabilities or individuals who are survivors of accidents or crimes. Yet, I have worked hard to recognize that rehabilitation and adapting was an empowering development in both my physical and mental health. I remember when the movie "Finding Nemo" came out and the discovery of Dory (who also had cognitive disabilities) chanted and sang "just keep swimming." This is exactly how PTG works. One does not ignore or deny the challenge. Instead one recognizes the opportunities the challenge provides, including the opportunity of growth. Once I adopted the mindset of PTG, less and less time was spent in feeling sorry for myself when disabilities worsened. My challenges are progressive. Understanding and accepting new limitations and adapting successfully was contingent on my having a growth mindset. Developing these domains in my personal growth ultimately helped me to become a catalyst of change in combating the microaggressions people with disability experience. These five domains are constantly referred to in my writing at "Hearing Elmo" (Portis, 2022).

CONCLUSION

Two quotes are written on post-it notes and hang in various places in my workspaces. Dr. King Jr. (2010) said, "The ultimate measure of a man is not where he stands in moments of comfort and convenience, but where he stands at times of challenge and controversy" (p. 26). It reminds me that I am who I am; a person with a disability who by being differently abled is in fact, a person of influence. A second Post-itTM note has written Helen Keller's (1927/2000) words, "The marvelous richness of human experience would lose something of rewarding joy if there were no limitations to overcome. The hilltop hour would not be half so wonderful if there were no dark valleys to traverse" (p. 121). Both quotes remind me that my disabilities and challenges are important aspects of self-development and success. I believe adjuncts with a disability can identify intrinsic workplace factors that emerge from their involvement in training, advocacy, and example leadership and that by doing so improve job satisfaction and personal growth.

REFERENCES

American Psychological Association. (n.d.). *Disability mentoring program.* Retrieved June 21, 2022, from https://www.apa.org/pi/disability/resources/mentoring

American Psychological Association. (2020). Bias-free language guidelines. In *Publication manual of the American Psychological Association: The official guide to APA style* (7th 3d.; pp. 131–149).

Bogart, K. R., Bonnett, A. K., Logan, S. W., & Kallem, C. (2022). Intervening on disability attitudes through disability models and contact in psychology education. *Scholarship of Teaching and Learning in Psychology, 8*(1), 15–26. https://doi.org/10.1037/stl0000194

Calhoun, L. G., & Tedeschi, R. G. (2014). Foundations of posttraumatic growth. In L. Calhoun & R. Tedeschi (Eds.), *Handbook of posttraumatic growth: Research and practice* (pp. 3–21). Psychology Press

Centers for Disease Control and Prevention. (2020). *Disability and health promotion: Disability impacts all of us.* Retrieved June 16, 2022, from https://www.cdc.gov/ncbddd/disabilityandhealth/infographic-disability-impacts-all.html

Dirth, T. P., & Branscombe, N. R. (2018). The social identity approach to disability: Bridging disability studies and psychological science. *Psychological Bulletin, 144*(12), 1300–1324. https://doi.org/10.1037/bul0000156

Freedberg, L. (2022, April 4). *Post-pandemic, will community college students keep choosing online instruction?* EDSource. https://edsource.org/2022/post-pandemic-will-community-college-students-keep-choosing-online-instruction/669761

Goodley, D. (2017). *Disability studies: An interdisciplinary introduction* (2nd ed.). SAGE Publications.

Halder, S., & Assaf, L. C. (Ed.). (2017). *Inclusion, disability and culture: An ethnographic perspective traversing abilities and challenges.* Springer International Publishing.

Jackson, L. M. (2020). *The psychology of prejudice: From attitudes to social Action* (2nd ed.). American Psychological Association.

Keller, H. (2000). *Light in my darkness* (Silverman, R., Ed.). Chrysalis Books. (Original work published 1927).

King, M. L., Jr. (2010). *Strength to love.* Fortress Press. (Original work published 1963)

Ladau, E. (2021). *Demystifying disability: What to know, what to say, and how to be an ally.* Ten Speed Press.

Morris, J. (1996). *Pride against prejudice: Transforming attitudes to disability.* The Women's Press.

Portis, L. D. (2022, June 18). I would rather walk with a friend in the dark, than alone in the light. *Wordpress.* http://hearing-elmo.com/2018/06/01/i-would-rather-walk-with-a-friend-in-the-dark-than-alone-in-the-light/

Tedeschi, R. G., Shakespeare-Finch, J., Taku, K., & Calhoun, L. G. (2018). *Posttraumatic growth: Theory, research, and applications*. Routledge.

U.S. Department of Health and Human Services. (2021). *Civil rights: Guidance on "Long COVID" as a disability under the ADA, Section 504, and Section 1557*. Retrieved June 19, 2022, from https://www.hhs.gov/civil-rights/for-providers/civil-rights-covid19/guidance-long-covid-disability/index.html

U.S. Department of Labor. (n.d.). *Youth, disclosure, and the workplace why, when, what, and how*. Retrieved June 20, 2022, from https://www.dol.gov/agencies/odep/publications/fact-sheets/youth-disclosure-and-the-workplace-why-when-what-and-how

Zippia: The Career Expert. (2022). *Adjunct faculty member demographics and statistics in the US*. Retrieved June 17, 2022, from https://www.zippia.com/adjunct-faculty-member-jobs/demographics/

CHAPTER 2

WHAT THEY WON'T TELL YOU

Dos and Don'ts to Adjuncting While in the Academe

Leslie Ekpe
Ashlee Daniels
Sylviane Greensword

ABSTRACT

So, you want to adjunct? Well, there are some things you need to know while teaching in the academy. The focus of this chapter is to provide the dos and don'ts to navigating the academy as an adjunct. It is critical as an adjunct to recognize one's role as a faculty member related to the importance of networking, prioritizing, and safeguarding oneself. To best illuminate our experiences, we utilize the practice of collaborative autoethnography (Chang, 2013), which allows us to highlight the similarities and differences in our experiences that ultimately contribute to our roles as adjuncts at the institutions we serve. Through storytelling, we honor the traditions of documenting our culturally informed lived experiences (Owens et al., 2019). Lastly, we provide recommendations for adjuncts and institutions based on our stories.

Don't Forget About the Adjuncts!, pages 13–25
Copyright © 2023 by Information Age Publishing
www.infoagepub.com
All rights of reproduction in any form reserved.

13

As a professional, you might be looking to diversify your expertise through adjuncting or add another stream of income to your finances. Whether a monetary decision or expanding career opportunities, adjuncting or part-time teaching offers a wide range of possibilities; in this, if adjuncting is something that you are interested in, there are a couple of things you need to know. Adjuncting should not be seen as an easy job position. Frequently, adjunct faculty are financially, mentally, and emotionally exploited within higher education systems (Rhoades, 2020). In most cases, adjunct faculty are faced with unrealistic job expectations and outcomes (Nica, 2018). Thus, these faculty members have limited opportunities to assist in institutional governance, fewer chances for funding support, as well as receiving no health insurance benefits (Brennan & Magness, 2018). Unrealistic expectations have a direct impact on those adjunct faculty who wish to matriculate into a tenured faculty role (Nica, 2018). This chapter aims to shed light on the dos and don'ts of adjuncting while in the academy and provides encouragement and tips to current and future faculty in these positions.

There are more part-time-based faculty within higher education than ever before. In American higher education, part-time faculty has grown to almost half of all faculty (Nica, 2018). Moreover, there has been an increasing number of students at the postsecondary level, but not an equal increase in full-time faculty. Although part-time faculty are now a significant component of American colleges and universities, there is little information available about their membership, so they cannot be adequately addressed. It is also important to note that the percentage of full-time faculty is drastically decreasing. That being so, as the foundation of higher education continues to change, colleges and universities must consider the support needed for adjuncts to succeed in the academy. Thus, it is critical to ensure part-time faculty can benefit from the university's resources.

COLLABORATIVE AUTOETHNOGRAPHY

The approach we took to this chapter is a collaborative autoethnography which highlights our personal experiences as adjuncts in the academy. Ellis and Bochner (2000) state that a collaborative autoethnography approach "allow readers to feel moral dilemmas, [to] think with our story instead of about it" (p. 735). A qualitative method of research, autoethnography involves collecting, analyzing, and interpreting autobiographical data to obtain a cultural understanding of how self is connected to others. Chang (2008) describes autoethnography as a method for gathering, analyzing, and interpreting the personal narratives of researchers. Throughout this chapter, we employed a concurrent approach to collaboration (Chang, 2013). We do this by combining individual narratives with greater collective experiences. Collaborative ethnography explores shared stories and creates a balance between the individual narratives (Blalock & Akehi, 2018). This chapter reflects our shared autoethnography and respects one another's stories, allowing us to contribute personal and unique memories and experiences. The collaborative autoethnography approach also highlights our distinct experiences as adjuncts, as we were aware that they were essential to honoring that shared dialogue and sharing our stories.

COLLABORATIVE AUTOETHNOGRAPHIC NARRATIVES

Tuckman (1978) and Gappa and Leslie (1993) found considerable variation in motivations among part-time faculty. Schuster and Finkelstein (2006) state, "The part-time professoriate has at once grown explosively and continues to represent a wide diversity of motivations, commitments, and qualifications" (p. 411). Using collaborative autoethnography, we can extend discussions about the psychological effects of systems, policies, and social ties by explicitly using narratives and qualitative research more generally (Ellis, 2009). As Black women adjuncts, we found solace in illuminating one another through our shared narratives relating to adjuncting in the postsecondary realm. In light of our academic interests and personal experiences as Black women academics, we sought to better recommend the dos and don'ts for those wanting to join the adjunct community.

Leslie

More Than an Educator

Leslie has over 7 years of experience as an adjunct. She is a PhD candidate in the higher educational leadership program at her university. Her goal is to continue in the academy as a professor teaching anti-racism and social justice coursework.

As an adjunct, I am always looking for ways to develop myself for the betterment of my students. In this, I knew it was important to network in order to propel myself into my career. Although adjuncts are not given the number of resources that full-time faculty are afforded, I still make it an objective to utilize the resources I am given while seeking out additional resources that will assist me in teaching. I first began my adjuncting at the university level in 2016, where I began teaching at a community college. I had no idea what to expect, but all I knew was that I wanted to teach students the importance of education and how to use education as a foundation to propel them into their careers. Sounds pretty straightforward, right? Well, to my surprise, it is much more than that. On the first day of class, I

16 ▪ L. EKPE, A. DANIELS, and S. GREENSWORD

was thrown into my class with not as many resources as needed. When asked questions by the students, I was, for the most part, underprepared as it related to the question(s) being asked. On top of this, many of the students were not prepared as well. Because we were in a technology laboratory (a room in which desktop computers were stationed on each of the student's desks), students thought they would not need any other items (syllabus, pencils, notebooks, etc.) in order to be prepared for class. I took fault in this because better communication was needed from me as the instructor to disseminate to my students. However, I truly did not know what was expected from me. The next couple of days were a whirlwind of getting to know my students, searching for personal development opportunities, and balancing my class schedule as it related to my teaching load. I quickly realized I was more than an educator. This meant that while students saw me as a teacher, and while I do serve in that role, I am also a mentor, a sister, a daughter, a believer, and so much more. A part of my identity is being an educator, but it is not my sole identity.

I wanted to become the best possible me throughout the process, so I reached out to a mentor who was a full-time faculty member to identify tips and tricks that I could adopt to become more stable in my adjunct practices. She told me, "There is no one way to do this. Each day comes with its own wins and challenges. But regardless of the win or challenge, never lose your focus." My mentor assisted me with finding my "Why?" I knew I was where I wanted to be, but I was struggling with developing my teaching philosophy because of encountering too many experiences with being unprepared. But my mentor's words began to stick with me as I worked on developing a plan for approaching my teaching. Fast forward a few years later, as I continue to work diligently towards becoming a better educator each day; I am 100% committed to assisting other adjuncts in their needs to fulfill their roles. I do this by actively practicing habits that contribute to the decolonization of White supremacist structures in order to invite and illuminate voices that have traditionally been excluded from the conversation. Because of my intricate experiences, I believe in the Sankofa practice of "reaching back." Just as my mentor helped me with navigating the dos and don'ts of adjuncting, I want to extend the same hand I was given to those wishing to adjunct.

Ashlee

Mr. Feeny From "Boys Meet World"

Ashlee is a lecturer in the English department at her university. With over 8 years combined of experience teaching at both the K–12 and postsecondary levels, Ashlee looks to continue the work of educating after gaining her doctorate through a think-tank route.

In high school, I was a student who was on grade level; however, in some instances, I felt alienated from my peers as I did not do well on standardized tests. So, instead of allowing my classmates to see my failure, I behaved poorly and did not participate in in-class exercises. I regret my behavior; however, I do not regret the experience because it has made me aware of my potential as an educator. Academic learning should never be seen as a punishment but as a gift. I understood that I could do nothing to change the system alone, so I transitioned into teaching in higher education to provide insight to students just like me entering college—underprepared and provided limited resources to be successful in the first year of college. However, the challenges I would face as an adjunct faculty sometimes derailed me from my mission.

I wanted to be Mr. Feeny from "Boys Meet World" and having multiple enlightened moments with my students every semester while striving to be the perfect adjunct began to affect me in various ways. Clearly, that was a false fantasy on my part. Because of structures and practices in higher education that can make you feel you are not doing enough as an educator, it can sometimes be easy to compare yourself to others; creating a practice of competition to become what institutions deem as "perfect" or "acceptable." While I wanted to be the Buddha of education, the unrealistic job expectations of the position began to take a toll. Each semester I would take on 130 students—five sections of English level classes. I would assign a five-to-seven-page final research paper—as required in the course's student learning outcomes and was also tasked with needing to evaluate each student's paper within 1 week so that students can move on to the next assignment. I did not receive my degree in mathematics, but if each student wrote a max of seven pages, I would have to evaluate 910 pages within 1 week. So, let me be honest—the math was not "mathing" in the time management department. This example is one of many challenges I faced as an adjunct faculty; however, I did not let that stop me from achieving my goal in my career path and being of assistance to the students I serve. I developed ways to rethink my approaches to learning for the benefit of both my students and myself. Through nontraditional teaching approaches in class, I intentionally create space for everyone to be heard, seen, and valued. While we may not agree on everything, we can better grow from each other's thoughts and perspectives. The bonds that I create with my students each semester have outweighed any obstacles as an adjunct.

Sylviane

The Hunger Games

Sylviane is a postdoctoral fellow at her university. Sylviane is also a historian who studies the African Diaspora and the relation to translocalities and multiculturalism. In her work, Sylviane strives to decolonize practices in the academy that exclude Black and African American peoples.

My breakthrough occurred in 2020 when I was offered a postdoctoral position at my institution. I would be conducting ethnography, oral history, and archival research pertaining to the university's racial history. I accepted the position with the hope that it would lead to teaching opportunities. And it did. I was personally invited to apply for a 1-hour teaching assignment for a course as well. I was quite content because adjuncting is limited to teaching, and I have 15 years of teaching experience. I was able to focus on lesson delivery and lesson planning. I progressively moved to have my own course: Anthropology of *The Hunger Games.* Although I was an adjunct, my students called me Professor Greensword. I did not know how to correct them—or what difference it would make in their minds in their consideration or treatment of me. After all, one of the definitions of the word "professor" simply means "teacher at a college or university." I saw the opportunity to better disseminate knowledge around power structures. I want my students to understand while I may be the professor, we all hold the capacity to distribute awareness around critical issues.

The biggest challenges for me were:

1. *Balancing my teaching assignments with my other responsibilities.* To relieve some of the pressure and time constraints, I decided to integrate my postdoctoral work with my teaching. When teaching class, I incorporated my research on institutional history into my lessons on how to "experience the university" in students' first year. When teaching Anthropology of *The Hunger Games,* I paralleled my research with Suzanne Collins' cautionary tale against losing collective memory. On the other hand, while most adjuncts desire to achieve full-time faculty status, I value the fact that I am presently free from the pressure of publishing which affects so many of my colleagues. I write and submit my work, but I also know that my current job is not on the line based on whether my narratives get accepted or not. I now enjoy peace of mind that, once I transition to professorship, it will not be so accessible.

2. *My desire to excel as a teacher, given my pedagogical background, coupled with the comparatively greater freedom I was given in my lesson format and the students' freedom compared to my previous high school students.* In order to develop appropriate teaching skills, I was determined to utilize all resources that are also available to full-time faculty. I worked with our institutional center for instruction, innovation, and engagement to utilize rubrics to assess my own skills each year. I invited seasoned faculty to observe me and provide feedback. I have learned quite a lot throughout this time about my own

strengths and weaknesses. Being an adjunct has allowed me to focus on my growth as a teacher, and I know it will make a difference in my qualifications when I am ready to apply for full-time faculty positions.

3. *Balancing my family and work life.* Fortunately, my husband has gone through the experience of being a postdoc and a teacher, so he was most understanding of my demanding schedule and responsibilities. For my children, it was more complicated because they needed me to be entirely available to them: emotionally, mentally, and physically. What helped me was inviting them—especially the oldest four, who range between the ages of 8 and 13—into my world. I occasionally took them to campus with me and then discussed what they learned. These moments accounted for our bonding and sharing time. I got them copies of The Hunger Games series (Collins, 2008–2010), and to this day, we are still watching the movies and debating over the power of adaptation, as well as the ethical and cultural dilemmas raised in this work of fiction. They were also able to give me suggestions as to what they would like to see in their own classrooms, and I constantly use their insight as inspiration for my own lesson delivery.

WHAT THEY WON'T TELL YOU

Based on our experiences, it is critical to know that the adjuncting experience is not a monolithic experience. Everyone's experience will be different based on the institution you serve at, the classes you teach, and the students you serve. However, one thing remains constant, and that is you must be empowered to do this work. From our narratives and our cross-case analysis of analyzing themes that were consistent throughout our storytelling, we determined three dos and three don'ts for your success as an adjunct.

Dos

Network

Networking is critical to your role as an adjunct. The personal and professional networks you cultivate as an adjunct professor can be extremely valuable to you. A mentor or peer group can provide you with guidance during the difficult years when you may have to piece together jobs at multiple institutions. There is a general lack of investment by institutions of higher education in preparing contingent faculty for full-time employment. Full-time faculty are more likely able to invest sustained time in networking.

Nevertheless, adjuncts can remain abreast of key developments in the field by networking with other part-time faculty. Networking also allows you to develop your identity as an adjunct. The developmental opportunities you gain from networking will directly influence your identity as an adjunct and, in turn, establish your community on which you can rely. Despite the often-heavy workloads, instructors without institutional or formal support systems may neglect networking, a vital professional activity that is often ignored when workloads get heavy.

Prioritize

You must draft a game plan. Think of adjuncting like playing in the National Basketball Association (NBA) finals during game six. The pressure is on, and you know that you cannot step onto that court without a fireproof game plan. It is essential to create goals or objectives that focus on positive career outcomes and self-fulfillment at the beginning of each semester. The job responsibilities and duties of adjunct faculty can become daunting without proper planning and time management. So, we first must understand that we cannot control everything that happens at work. The only aspect we can control in every situation is ourselves; therefore, it is highly recommended to draft an objective game plan to tackle the semester. Drafting a game plan will prioritize the needs of the job without overextending yourself to do the impossible while also missing opportunities to move up the ladder in the academy. So, manifest your inner Chicago Bulls and play the game (i.e., the Bulls 1997 team, Jordan with the flu game, you get our point).

Safeguard

If you want to transition from adjunct to full-time faculty, safeguard your aspirations instead of settling for less. Keep up with the literature in your field and remain a part of the academic discussion. Remember, inside the classroom, most students do not distinguish between full-time faculty and adjunct faculty. Actually, most undergraduates could care less about their instructor's tenure status! Another area to safeguard is your home and your family life. Adjuncts are easily overwhelmed by a load of preparing lessons and grading papers. It is thus tempting to get home before rush hour and stay up late working at your dinner table—or worse, sitting in your bed. Our advice is to *leave work at work*. You will find that it is more efficient to arrive at work early than to stay at work late. Indeed, leaving your office—or your cubicle—early will give you a false sense that your workday is over. You will mentally clock out, but only to remain on the grind and work twice as hard to get back in the game, to the great frustration of those who see you but cannot enjoy your presence. Be mentally and emotionally available in every space you show up and that means taking care of you first.

Don'ts

Don't Crash and Burn

Adjuncting is like riding an emotional rollercoaster without seatbelts—you could crash and burn or, by a miracle, survive the semester unscathed. Finding a balance in prioritizing the objectives you would like to achieve in progressing your career while also sustaining the responsibilities and duties of your job position can become quite tedious. Without a proper plan, the fruits of your labor can reflect poorly on your individual annual evaluations. So, do not get caught up in the chaos of sustaining your job position while burning opportunities to progress your career. Also, beware of disregarding your job responsibilities to solely achieve your future career goals. If publishing research is one of your goals, make sure that you align the plan with the objectives of your department—for example, apply for conferences that align with your subject area and incorporate a lesson for your students that allows them to learn more about the conference. Lastly, provide feedback within your subject area to maintain the student learning objectives of the course while also building your research for said area. To avoid crash and burn circumstances, only say yes to what you can fully contribute to at the best of your abilities.

Don't Be Shy in Asking for Support

You only know what you know. While you may be new to the field, it never hurts to inquire about additional support through unacclaimed resources. Oftentimes, as a new adjunct, you may experience hesitancy in inquiring about additional resources, however, we are here to tell you, do not be afraid to ask. It is imperative that you receive the necessary resources to ensure your success as an adjunct. Sometimes this means stepping outside of your comfort zone to inquire about the resources that lead to opportunities.

Don't Forget About Benefits

We recommend that you research how adjunct benefits work at the schools you are interested in before applying. We advise doing your research on the front end, which will save you time and trouble. In addition to teaching part-time, benefits are one of the biggest barriers to working as an adjunct. If you can find an institution that offers solid healthcare coverage, you can do other things in addition to teaching part-time. Many part-time faculty members do not have access to health insurance, vacation days, or pension benefits due to their part-time positions (Jacoby, 2006). Part-time faculty may earn less per course than full-time faculty members and do not receive health or retirement benefits. As such, establishing your reasons for entering the adjunct field, and developing a benefits package that incorporates that, is vital to your well-being.

RECOMMENDATIONS

Furthermore, we leave recommendations for you as an adjunct that are critical to your success in the academy. These recommendations can also provide institutions with insight into factors that influence an adjunct's progress as an educator.

Tip and Strategy 1: Use Your Institutional Environment to Your Advantage

It is essential to become familiar with your work environment in any job position. Also, it is crucial to become familiar with the job requirements and expectations, as they can vary from each department in higher education. Adjuncts are a vital part of supporting institutions as there is an increase in the need for adjunct faculty new hires in contrast to tenured faculty (Morton, 2012; Caruth & Caruth, 2013). As an adjunct faculty, this means that you are valuable to the progression and innovation of your institution. Remember that they need you, so take advantage of this.

Start by first inquiring about your department's initiatives to determine if your game plan aligns with your personal goals and that of the department's—kind of like killing two birds with one stone (no animals were harmed in the writing of this chapter). Your game plan could likely receive support from the department in whatever capacity that may be. For example, if you are serving as adjunct faculty in the languages and communications department, it would not be beneficial to present a proposal about conducting rocket science to your department chair in hopes of support. Instead, try incorporating a student learning outcome of your assigned course and present your findings to your chair. Perhaps, rocket science is a little far-fetched. So, consider designing a proposal that incorporates a lesson in which students use critical thinking skills to learn about the sciences and apply them to composition.

Tip and Strategy 2: Strategize and Dominate Your Semester

For new and seasoned adjunct faculty, each semester can either make you or break you. No one likes the feeling of hanging on by a thread by the end of the semester. So, invoke your inner war hero, strategize, and dominate the battlefield for semesters to come. Adjunct faculty need effective support measures beyond orientation (Santisteban & Egues, 2014). However, research shows that adjunct faculty lack support and encouragement.

It is imperative to create your own fireproof plan so that you can manage obstacles that come your way. So, ask yourself, "Do I want to be a T-Rex or a goldfish this semester?"—the choice is yours.

Tip and Strategy 3: Maximize Your Time as an Adjunct

There is a false narrative that adjunct faculty cannot research, publish, or attend conferences due to either having a heavy workload or a lack of funding and support. Well, the narrative stands true for some; however, some adjunct faculty are successful by applying one key secret—maximizing their time while adjuncting. It is critical that you utilize your time wisely as an adjunct. Attend campus faculty meetings and learn what services are provided for faculty members on campus. Remember that you are a faculty member regardless of part-time or full-time status. Thus, you are entitled to some of the benefits provided by the institution. You could possibly surprise yourself and learn something new about your institution.

AFFIRMATIONS FOR ADJUNCTS

After providing you with the dos and don'ts of adjuncting based on our experiences, we want to ensure that we express how the world of adjuncting is truly rewarding. There is no better feeling than knowing you are making a direct impact on the future leaders of tomorrow. In this, remember to *empower* yourself in order to *empower* others. Fill yourself with the necessary components needed to be at your best so that you can empower those around you. Practice implementing the following:

A Checklist with a Fun Twist

Start your morning by drafting a short list of essential tasks you want to have accomplished that day. At the end of the day, add the extra things you were able to complete—no matter how small—and put a checkmark on them. Look at you! Accomplishing things! We see you! You betta!

Be Your Own Hypeman or Hypewoman

Before making a beeline from the parking lot to the office to start your workday, play that favorite song that really puts you in the zone. You are your biggest supporter, so make that 15–20 minute drive to work one that counts. Create a personal playlist of songs that will motivate you for the workday ahead—we highly recommend any of Beyonce's songs for novice and expert motivational listeners.

CONCLUSION

The key to making adjuncting work for you resides in your ability and determination to turn obstacles into advantages. Whether this position is your second (or third or fourth) career transition, or you are in graduate school, the flaw of the current higher education system (including the exploitation of adjuncts) is a lens through which you will be able to consider your own identity. In effect, the manner in which you navigate this system will bring to light your character flaws as well as your strengths: "Are you patient, driven, detail-oriented, sociable, and understanding as you always thought you were? Do your priorities and professional aspirations truly align?" This chapter was not so much about detailing the shortcomings of adjuncting or the higher education system but rather about bringing the focus back to *you*, our reader. How can you make adjunct instructorship work for *you*? Consider the perks of the job. Do not belittle yourself by constantly comparing yourself to full-time faculty. In the classroom and in the eyes of students—the population whom the entire system is designed to serve—you are a professor of your subject matter. You master both content and pedagogy, and you profess this knowledge in an academic setting. Do not discount this fact. Create a game plan and continue to develop your adjunct identity. The future depends on *you*.

REFERENCES

Blalock, A. E., & Akehi, M. (2018). Collaborative autoethnography as a pathway for transformative learning. *Journal of Transformative Education, 16*(2), 89–107. https://doi.org/10.1177/1541344617715711

Brennan, J., & Magness, P. (2018) Are adjunct faculty exploited: Some grounds for skepticism. *Journal of Business Ethics, 152*, 53–71. https://doi.org/10.1007/s10551-016-3322-4

Caruth, G. D., & Caruth, D. L. (2013). Adjunct faculty: Who are these unsung heroes of academe? *Current Issues in Education, 16*(3), 1–11.

Chang, H. (2008). *Autoethnography as method: Developing qualitative inquiry.* Left Coast Press.

Chang, H. (2013). Individual and collaborative autoethnography as method: A social scientist's perspective. In S. Holman Jones, T. E. Adams, & C. Ellis (Eds.), *Handbook of autoethnography* (pp. 107–122). Routledge.

Ellis, C., & Bochner, A. (2000). *Autoethnography, personal narrative, reflexivity: Researcher as subject.* https://www.researchgate.net/publication/254703924_Autoethnography_Personal_Narrative_Reflexivity_Researcher_as_Subject

Ellis, R. (2009). 1. Implicit and explicit learning, knowledge and instruction. In R. Ellis, S. Loewen, C. Elder, R. Erlam, J. Philp, & H. Reinders (Eds.), *Implicit and explicit knowledge in second language learning, testing and teaching* (pp. 3–26). Multilingual Matters.

Gappa, J. M., & Leslie, D. W. (1993). *The invisible faculty. Improving the status of part-timers in higher education.* Jossey-Bass Publishers.

Jacoby, D. (2006). Effects of part-time faculty employment on community college graduation rates. *The Journal of Higher Education, 77*(6), 1081–1103. https://doi.org/10.1080/00221546.2006.11778957

Morton, D. R. (2012). Adjunct faculty embraced: The institution's responsibility. *Christian Education Journal, 9*(2), 396. https://doi.org/10.1177/073989131200900211

Nica, E. (2018). Has the shift to overworked and underpaid adjunct faculty helped education outcomes? *Educational Philosophy and Theory, 50*(3), 213–216. https://doi.org/10.1080/00131857.2017.1300026

Owens, L., Edwards, E. B., & McArthur, S. A. (2019). Black women researchers' path to breaking silence: Three scholars reflect on voicing oppression, self-reflexive speech, and talking back to elite discourses. *Western Journal of Black Studies, 42*(3/4), 125–135. https://www.proquest.com/docview/2324919746

Rhoades, G. (2020). Taking college teachers' working conditions seriously: Adjunct faculty and negotiating a labor-based conception of quality. *The Journal of Higher Education, 91*(3), 327–352. https://doi.org/10.1080/00221546.2019.1664196

Santisteban, L., & Egues, A. L. (2014, July 1). Cultivating adjunct faculty: Strategies beyond orientation. *Nursing Forum, 49*(3), 152. https://doi.org/10.1111/nuf.12106

Schuster, J. H., & Finkelstein, M. J. (2006). *The American faculty: The restructuring of academic work and careers.* JHU Press.

Tuckman, H. P. (1978). Who is part-time in academe? *AAUP Bulletin, 64*(4), 305–315. https://doi.org/10.2307/40225146

CHAPTER 3

PRIORITIZING ADJUNCTS

Revisiting the Impact of Part-Time Educators, Leaders, and Entrepreneurs

Sierra JêCre McKissick

ABSTRACT

Although institutions claim the occupational hybridity adjuncts bring to academia is esteemed, discrepancies in access to resources like health care and job security remain. In this chapter, I will explore how adjuncts who serve as part-time faculty often bring additional experiential richness to academia and the cultural environment that contributes to the relevance of the institution and the practical application of theories and methods by its primary stakeholder: the students. While using jazz as a metaphor for the collaborative effort required between administration, tenured faculty, adjuncts, and students, I argue that in "not forgetting about the adjuncts," institutions should also be advocates for democratized learning and academic freedom that does not privilege or situate one's value to the institution based on professional career or affiliations alone but considers and seeks to expand one's collective capital and meaning (e.g., one's lived experience). I intend to use my personal experience in higher education grounded in a womanist-epistemic framework that honors lived experiences and disrupts the colonial matrix of power.

Don't Forget About the Adjuncts!, pages 27–41
Copyright © 2023 by Information Age Publishing
www.infoagepub.com
All rights of reproduction in any form reserved.

27

28 · S. J. McKISSICK

I decided we must do something about this latest outrage,
even as many of the people to whom we felt close ran away
to join the mbeles *or forest people, who live deep in the jungle,*
refusing to work for whites or be ruled by them.

—Excerpt from Nettie's letter in the book *The Color Purple*
(Walker, 2003, p. 231)

Higher education in America has done several things well. In addition to the list that most stakeholders in education would draft, I would add that higher education has always benefited from licensing knowledge from those committed to changing the world. In 1970, there were 369,000 full-time faculty and 104,000 part-time faculty employed in institutions across the United States (National Center for Education Statistics, 2016). By 2015, there were 807,032 full-time faculty and 743,983 part-time (National Center for Education Statistics, 2016). More so in its latter years, American higher education has rebuilt its academic curriculum and relevance on the backs of adjunct faculty—especially people of color—while labeling their contribution as "important," and their commitment "part time." One of the most challenging assessments for adjunct faculty to accept is how the work of serving as an instructor can be labeled part time when in reality, the fullness of their service is parallel to the load of full-time faculty.

In addition to managing the needs demanded from designing one course or more, teaching students, holding office hours, and grading; adjunct faculty who maintain career employment outside of their teaching institution manage multiple roles, skill sets, and professional assignments. Moreover, institutions must admit the increase in adjunct faculty was based on the need to alleviate the governance responsibilities held by full-time or tenured faculty while maintaining an academic hierarchy and protecting power over resources (i.e., healthcare, funding, job security, etc.). Academics have long criticized the adoption of capitalistic practices in academia and debated the placement of adjuncts and their temporary role within higher education. According to a researcher at the American Association of University Professors, "Under academic capitalism the focus is shifting from the faculty as a community of self-governing scholars to the faculty as a collection of individual entrepreneurs" (Reichman, 2020, para. 22). For adjuncts, financial security cannot always be achieved in a singular teaching position. Adjuncts are educators as well as leaders within their communities, caretakers in their homes, and survivors of circumstance. Sharing the title "entrepreneur" is appropriate given the risks adjuncts take to design tools that improve the quality of life many people experience and create an imprint on industries that will last for generations.

My comments regarding the similar intensity of managing teaching and outside employment roles should not be seen as an opportunity to remove the privilege of serving as an instructor from adjuncts with more than one position or interpreted and simplified as a burden. I mention this as a reminder that adjuncts' identities are as complex as tenured faculty. It is plausible tenured faculty in higher education might question adjunct faculty's capacity to manage both and insist they choose one career pathway over the other. However, revoking teaching opportunities to those who hold career employment outside of the institution and insisting adjuncts choose one pathway is an unhelpful response and ignores what remains at the core of this and other issues within higher education. Higher education misdiagnoses issues situated in a lack of equity as isolated incidents involving overly ambitious personnel, which has allowed this untruth to continue marginalizing people who desire to contribute to higher education, but have not been permitted to join the select group of scholars.

Despite the selective inclusion of marginalized peoples, American higher education institutions continue to cling to the colonial matrix of power that makes access to education exclusive and profitable. In this chapter, I will explore how adjuncts who serve as part-time faculty often bring additional experiential richness to academia and the cultural environment that contributes to the relevance of the institution and the practical application of theories and methods by its primary stakeholder: the students. As a scholar deeply invested in womanist and practical theology as well as ethics, I employ the wisdom of these disciplines while addressing the challenges and opportunities I have experienced and continue conversations surrounding social epistemology and racial capitalism. Since womanism is committed to the survival of all people and the act of allowing people of color to speak from their experiences and share their own stories as an act of resistance, it justly serves as the methodological lens for this conversation concerning my experiences within higher education (Walker, 1984). In using this methodology, I intend to measure the impact of adjunct faculty using public testimonials and personal course evaluations. Last, in arguing for institutions to advocate for democratized learning and academic freedom through the prioritization of adjunct faculty and their needs, I explore the musical style known as *jazz* as a metaphor for the collaboration, improvisation, and the consent necessary in order for adjunct instructors to be impactful within academia.

LEARNING TO PLAY THE GAME

While completing the second year of my master's program I could have continued on to doctoral studies, despite this I chose not to apply. An instructor for a clinical seminar course in my program shared her personal frustration while serving as a nontenured assistant professor of practice seeking tenure status. She, a White woman in her 50s or early 60s, explained that earning credentials and working endlessly was part of *playing the game.* Realizing that, at the time, I had completed 9 years consecutively in higher education and was no longer interested in "the game," I withdrew. I had obtained enough credentials to serve as an adjunct instructor for undergraduate religious studies and was willing to take my chances of being hired. While the process for applying and interviewing for teaching positions was foreign to me, I considered the challenge part of the new journey I was designing for myself. Prior to becoming an adjunct instructor, I served as a teaching assistant for two tenured faculty members at separate institutions. One was a White male English professor teaching a gaming course and the other a Black female psychology professor overseeing an independent study course. Each course presented a different experience for me as a Black woman in my early twenties assisting esteemed professors both over 50 years old. I quickly realized that predetermined syllabus and recycled lecture notes were the crutch that made teaching in higher education repeatable, although not always effective. When I received the position as an adjunct instructor, my primary concern was to not become too disruptive. As a Black woman in the Bible Belt perimeter of the South, teaching Christian religious studies rooted in justice and honoring marginalized identities at a private, predominantly White institution could potentially cause unwarranted conflict and physical danger. In using methodologies that rely on challenging perspectives surrounding race and freedom, I often stand in opposition of popular White southern politics that would support White privilege and theological interpretations that underpin opinions on abortion, enslavement, and human sexuality. In doing so, I have had to withstand verbal disagreements during meetings with colleagues, vicious emails from students and parents, and suggestive body language that made me uncomfortable. My ethnicity, gender, and economic background is not muted in the spaces I enter within higher education. To do so is to dishonor the experiences and lives that brought me here.

During my initial interview, the dean made it clear that my identity as a Black woman and, at the time, blogger made me a competitive candidate for the position. He noted that students held an interest in building an online brand and that my experience could aid in cultivating their knowledge and ability to utilize mainstream resources in their professional careers. Once employed, I used these very skills to unearth students' untapped potential and draw connections between their personal and professional lives and academic studies. I currently teach two courses in Christian religious studies. The first is an introduction to understanding the Bible for incoming students and the second is a junior cornerstone philosophy of religion course. Each course has allowed me to wield various tools from my roles as a multi-hyphenate creator and educator, yet, I do not achieve it without challenges. Before continuing, I think it is important to note that since I left the graduate program, the instructor for the clinical seminar course retired after not receiving a tenured position. The belief that playing the game could secure one's professional safety in academia or that success is possible for anyone who tries is entirely false (Townes & Cannon, 2021).

Regrettably, higher education remains an institution committed to the perpetuation of elitism through the management of power over the organization itself, personnel, and resources (Robichaud & Crevier, 2016). Institutions often suggest explicitly and implicitly that they have no desire to alter their operational structure and forfeit the increase in cultural and economic capital regardless of whether it is deeply rooted in the oppression of students and staff (Robichaud & Crevier, 2016). This vein of thought was made evident once more when institutions refused to offer online courses during the 2020 outbreak of COVID-19 despite student petitions and protest from faculty. Institutions who chose to ignore the risk standard course sizes presented were negligent and reckless. Although I had transitioned to teaching online prior to the pandemic, I shared the frustration of colleagues who were afraid for their health and the health of our students and community. Adjunct instructors, many who taught introductory courses, were expected to proceed with instruction while 30 or more students were in class or decline their course load for the academic year. Unfortunately, the risk has not subsided and I remain saddened by higher education's collective response to the health crisis. The pandemic was and remains an outcry for administrations across all industries to confront and change the demands placed on critical personnel and the ways their health is put at risk. Together, we must examine why this sacrifice is permitted in systemic management within academic spaces as the rule, not the exception. Confronting the colonial matrix of power within higher education requires that its leadership admit to benefiting from elite educational culture and allowing it to dominate our educational values at the expense of its instructors and students. Furthermore, while learning what it means to play the game one must recognize the rules to the game can be revised at the discretion of the benefactor and will likely compromise the very players it should protect.

TOO MUCH FREEDOM, TOO SOON

Serving as an instructor in higher education is a beautiful challenge of thought, communication, and—for people of color—restraint. While higher education has remained male dominated, a 2018 online study conducted by the Teachers Insurance and Annuity Association of America (TIAA Institute) found that 70% of adjuncts are over Age 40, and 52% are women (Yakoboski, 2018). In addition to a little more than half of adjunct faculty

32 • S. J. McKISSICK

being women, adjuncts under Age 40 are more likely to be dissatisfied with their career, as are those with a PhD (Yakoboski, 2018). As an instructor who falls in the category of being under Age 40 and a woman, I have three issues concerning this data that address the challenges I have experienced as an adjunct instructor. The first is quite obvious in that although institutions are pursuing gender-based diversity, there is a clear restriction on what type of women are allowed employment based on age, degree level, and accomplishments. My statement earlier in this chapter concerning being too disruptive addresses this very fact. Human beings acquire knowledge through culture, most often obtaining it through the culture into which we are born. As Janette Taylor (1998) explains, "The simultaneous influence of class, race, and gender is not constant but changes according to life events" (p. 55). As an essential component of human existence, women have always participated and served as pioneers in the production of knowledge. Our knowledge flows from the experiences we have survived while existing in a patriarchal society that refuses to acknowledge the intricacy and divine wholeness of our womanhood. I exist within a field that remains predominantly male and where women exist, they are White women unaware of the Black experience. I have had to prove that personal experiences and other people's experience of poverty, violence, racial and gender discrimination have a right to exist within my research, curriculum, and conversations. Witnessing physical and sexual violence as youth and being falsely accused of stealing from a grocery store at 21 influences my work. It is a significant part of my identity as a woman. Being a Black woman in religious studies with a speciality in womanist pastoral theology and care for young adults of color is a niche within a field that is "undernourished" and "lacks representation" (Sheppard, 2011, p. 42).

In the snippet taken from *The Color Purple* (Walker, 2003) that introduces this chapter, Nettie's letter to Celie signals a call to action in response to the English authorities that are acquiring control over the Africans and have taken their ancestral rights. Although Nettie, characterized as a traveler and an intelligent Black woman, has felt like an outsider among the Africans and will later return to America, she carries her experiences, her stories, her writings, and her declaration that something must be done about universal oppression with her. Womanist thought demands that all women's, specifically Black women's, experiential differences should be seriously considered, taken as truth, and turned into action that liberates them from all forms of oppression. It is the essence of perspectival differences––"the who we are because of what we have survived"—that in turn carries epistemic consequences. Higher education admits that this thoughtful and transformative reaction is valuable, and yet, under rewards its alchemist. Similar to Nettie, I enthusiastically embarked on a journey hoping to find comradery among other intellectuals and discovered that higher education

Prioritizing Adjuncts • **33**

shared many of the oppressive perspectives found in the dominant society and was not structured to support expectations concerning freedom like epistemic autonomy, let alone mentorship. I carry the charge that I am within higher education because something must be done to change how we learn, and yet, I remain concerned that if too much of my identity shows up in my work and conflicts with the evolving opinions of colleagues or students, it could end in misfortune. My work is centered on my "being in" an institution and my critical reflection is celebrated by my community because it grants them access to understanding how institutions work while it simultaneously poses a threat to my position within the institution I critique. As an adjunct, if I tread too heavily, it would cost me dearly.

When I was hired as an adjunct, I was the only Black woman in my department. During the onboarding process the dean mentioned that I would have a mentor, but after the first semester and a few reminders on my end, no one contacted me. I attended conferences and events without any concern from the department. To my advantage, other faculty did not see me as a threat or in need of immediate professional development. My invisibility made it painfully obvious that I was one of the first Black people and Black women to teach in the department. It was not until a White male student challenged my instruction in front of my entire class I realized something must be done to correct the passive response that was silencing my presence and authority. As a former student with 9 years of experience, I knew that this would never happen to an older tenured professor who was White and male. Despite my position of authority, the student challenged me on the belief that he had completed the assignment correctly and deserved a higher grade. His concern was not based on his confidence in understanding the course material but rooted in his entitlement and desire to maintain his scholarship and high grade point average. Thus, he believed he could publicly pressure me to alter my decision. He claimed that I whimsically graded assignments based on my feelings about their argument rather than having a clear criterion. After addressing his inappropriate behavior publicly and privately clarifying how he completed the assignment incorrectly and ignored the outline listed in the syllabus, he was disgruntled, but retreated. Unfortunately, this experience of violence isn't uncommon for women, especially women of color within academia. Likewise, fearing employer retribution as a result of students' displeasure, rest at the forefront of our engagement in the academy.

We carry the bitter truth that Black people are not given the luxury of being automatically respected or believed. Katie Cannon (2006) clarifies that, for Black people, "mental anguish, physical abuse, and emotional agony are all part of the lived truth of Black people's straitened circumstance" (p. 3). Standing your ground when challenged, attending conferences unprepared, meeting in rooms with one exit, walking through the parking

34 • S. J. McKISSICK

garage at night or taking an alleyway after class, being emotionally moved to tears, or responding impulsively are not actions we can perform without simultaneously considering how it could place us in danger. In the past 7 years, I've known five women of color to terminate their enrollment in doctoral programs and teaching positions because they refused to endure the violence done to them by advisors, committee members, and colleagues. Their resistance and response to oppressive attitudes put an end to allowing institutions to count them as members of the community while limiting their participation to what they deemed nonthreatening behaviors. When an institution claims it is searching for ways to correct sexual, religious, racial, and gender-based disparities, it should also consider how the institution has been prepped to create environmental and social security for these identities to live and be respected. Meeting the diversity quota is meaningless if the livelihood of those seen as different is constantly in danger.

The second issue to be addressed using these findings is the financial challenges adjunct instructors face while teaching. While the average compensation rate per course is $3,000, 65% of single adjuncts report household income of less than $50,000 (Yakoboski, 2018). This means on a regular salary adjuncts would be paid $7.50 per hour to work 5 to 7 days per week. It is important to emphasize this hourly rate is less than what a McDonald's employee would be paid for working the drive thru service. The financial challenges adjuncts face should not be disregarded simply because they have not earned a doctorate degree, worked at the institution long enough, or been selected for a tenure-track position. If adjuncts are going to be seen as professionals who offer valuable instruction in areas that supplement the core pedagogical instruction, the adjunct's personhood and the experiential history and resources the adjunct brings should be treated as such. Again, this is not solely a complaint about the compensation rate adjuncts receive, but a call to acknowledge the importance labeling has on one's financial health and access to resources. Although when the majority of the teaching faculty is adjuncts who make $3,000 per 3- to 5-month course, it is reasonable to suggest the compensation package protect the labor and health of all people who aid in keeping the institution afloat. In addition to the compensation rate, adjunct faculty do not receive health care or retirement benefits because they are considered part-time employees.

Recently, I was scheduled to teach my standard course with approximately 30 students enrolled and even received emails from students expressing their excitement for the course. A few weeks before the course was scheduled to begin, the dean informed me that due to decreases in enrollment the course was to be reassigned to a full-time faculty member. He apologized, assuring me that this was not a disciplinary consequence and confessed it was the first time he had ever had to take this action. Through his apologies it was clear someone more essential to the department needed the course, and he was obligated to comply. While it is possible there were additional factors or policies that led to this outcome, as an educator whose primary income is from teaching, I was numb and concerned about how I would survive. Typically, I arrange my finances to ensure my spring semester compensation lasts January through September. However, with my course being reassigned I had to cover 8 months of financial responsibilities. The American Association of University Professors reported hearing tales of adjuncts on food stamps, sleeping in cars, or even dying of preventable medical conditions because they lacked the benefits of a full-time permanent position (Reichman, 2020). As an adjunct, I manage the anxiety of knowing that my health and career is at the mercy of the department and that mercy is given and taken at their pleasure.

The third issue is both a challenge and a benefit of serving as an adjunct. Being an active instructor demands that adjuncts strive to meet the outcomes set for the course, while allowing students to add to those outcomes by sharing their journeys and interpretations of their transformations while learning. This is a difficult task to complete if the adjunct's sole focus is on doing rather than being. Alastair Campbell (2005) describes the *courageous shepherd* as someone who has "entered into the darkness of another's pain, loss, or bewilderment and who has done so without defenses of detached professionalism" (p. 54). Without question, I cherish the privilege of shepherding students through their journey of intellectual development and connecting students to their current truths. As an instructor, we have the opportunity to present novel information to students and watch their transformation, for better or worse, however, it is not easy. After sharing films or course readings I have spoken to students who were triggered and able to recall memories they had long forgotten. I have listened to stories of homesickness, substance abuse, physical and spiritual abuse, the pain of divorce, and the hope that having an education might liberate students from poverty.

To serve as an adjunct is not a part-time commitment, but a lifelong willingness to bear witness and labor alongside others in a community. Kyle Carrero Lopez (2022) comically reflected on his college experience on Twitter writing, "Academia loves to establish hierarchy with titles like 'visiting assistant just-poppin-in associate substitute non-senior junior varsity' professor" in another tweet he continued,

> Most of the profs [*sic*] who really changed my life in undergrad were ones with titles like these, usually working in younger or more "fringe" fields, serious, generous scholars who lacked nothing other than tenure and years teaching in one place.

Although the work of adjuncts might be taken less seriously by some, many adjuncts would agree to take pride in being able to pay homage

36 ▪ S. J. McKISSICK

and forward histories within our fields with respect and vigor. Much like Paul Farmer's (2005) description, bearing witness is a task that needs to be done for the sake of the dead and forgotten. For a womanist, bearing witness is an integral part of lamenting and liberating others who have been dismissed while helping them journey back to the "human family" (Townsend Gilkes, 1997, p. 276).

Although I have experienced painful moments of invisibility in higher education, I have also experienced optimum moments of delight that affirmed my power of influence and presence within higher education. In January 2019, a student emailed me sharing her final thoughts about the course during the previous semester. She wrote,

> Professor McKissick,
>
> I was in your eight week Understanding the Bible class on Monday nights last semester. I wanted to reach out and let you know what an impact your class has had on me.
>
> I am a freshman from Indiana. Although I am not too far from home, adjusting to college has been a painful process. Most of that stems from the extremely close bonds my family shares with one another. Due to my struggle, school was especially difficult.
>
> As a result, I did not walk into your class very hopeful. In fact, I despised the thought of a four-hour night class. To make things even better, I had been feeling very overwhelmed about religion. It was the last thing I wanted to talk about.
>
> However, I was pleasantly surprised. I grew more in your class than any other class last semester. I rarely talk in group settings, but I found myself constantly sharing in your class. The strangest part was I did not feel forced. Instead, I had this urge to share. For the first time in any class I actually wanted to talk. Not only did I find myself sharing in person, but in my papers. I have never had the freedom to write like we did in your class. Through the writing assignments I found myself pouring out hard events I had experienced. Although it was difficult to share and explain, it was extremely cathartic.
>
> Last semester I grew as a person and student in incredible ways, but your class was the icing on the cake. Today, I have a new perspective on learning. I have discovered the power of making connections to material. In fact, I was so fascinated by class that I would call my mom on my walk home to fill her in.
>
> I cannot fully explain how powerful this experience was to me. Although it was only eight weeks, the knowledge I gained will stay with me. Today, it helps me put things into [*sic*] and accept expression in my writing. Thank you so much for opening my mind to the world around me including religion, life, expression, and learning.
>
> (Student, personal communication, January 15, 2018)

Designing courses that allow students the intellectual safety necessary to embody their own ways of thinking and being is by far one of the greatest opportunities I have as an educator. During our transition to online learning due to the pandemic, students were concerned with feeling isolated and being unable to understand assignments taught online. I did my best to offer options for assignments that required actions they regularly do with technologies. For example, sharing narratives using Instagram stories and posting to our classroom feed in Google groups.

SUPPORTING COURAGEOUS ADJUNCTS

At the end of the semester, students were asked to describe the most helpful or effective aspect of the course using an anonymous evaluation. Students' feedback indicated their satisfaction with the organization of my course, but more importantly my openness to allowing them freedom to craft and appreciate their own thinking and writing. As an instructor, your efforts to impart knowledge will be most effective when you create space for the knowledge students bring into the classroom as well as your own. As shepherds and guides to understanding, we cannot allow transformations to occur haphazardly and without creating safety in the classroom. It is important to remember as you create an imbalance by sharing new information students are searching their own canon for wisdom. You will disrupt belief systems and deep-rooted pathological beliefs that have previously protected students and helped them make meaning out of their lives. Be cautious and aware that significant places, people, and powerful relationships link us to our beliefs and when they are disrupted, they must be replaced. In 2017, when I chose to end my time as a student in higher education, my mother sought to affirm my choice and assure me I had achieved my purpose at the time by saying, "Sierra, you went to school to learn how to learn; you did that." I have carried this message in my heart to encourage me to push forward on days I feel empowered and soothe feelings of inadequacy, frustration, and failure on days I'm filled with unbelief about the profession. It is my reminder that education should be accessible, because it is a means of survival.

In addition to relationships with students, another opportunity has been to develop an archive of stories with colleagues in the thick of this journey and share with friends who ask questions like, "Do students care about religion these days?" It is with delight that I can defend the moments of discovery we create in the classroom and mention the changes students have made in their immediate world. Having colleagues that challenge you to write, to continue studying, serving, and surviving while disrupting corruption in higher education, congregations, and communities is holiness in action. Every day I serve as an adjunct is full of endless possibilities and opportunities to create

38 • S. J. McKISSICK

something new and intentionally revisit something old, to mine its ruins for hope to continue forward with a vision of true freedom.

DREAMING IN RETROSPECT

Much of this chapter has focused on addressing the challenges I and other adjuncts face in the field, however, this conversation would be unfinished without offering upcoming and current adjunct faculty wisdoms for successfully navigating the field. In truth, every institution presents its own ecosystem of rituals and challenges, but the ones I have mentioned are typically universal. In knowing this, the greatest wisdom I can share is to remind instructors that every institution is flawed, and a good student studies the information that is and is not available to them. It is rare that I finish a class session that does not challenge students to consider what is missing. Whether it is the experiences of marginalized groups, a footnote, or a closer description of a supporting character in a novel. I challenge students to notice what is seen and unseen. In doing so, my intention is to strengthen their critical thinking in the hope each student is able to better understand themselves, their motivations, and goals. Potential and current adjunct faculty should do the same with their lives while taking time to reflect on their personal and professional experiences and locate spaces where they are invited to share narratives while constructively critiquing spaces that deny them the opportunity to do so. Take on the task of writing your most vivid experiences in third person narrative and include specific details when possible. Then, list the names of people and places where you have felt safe and able to exist freely. This strategic exercise will provide you with a roadmap of soulless spaces where your voice and experiences are needed and spaces you can go for refuge when the fight for freedom or justice seems overwhelming. Audre Lorde (2018) confesses that those of us "forged in the crucibles of differences" know that "survival is not an academic skill" (pp. 18–19). The academy cannot be your home. For members of groups who have had to survive poverty, discrimination, and violence, we occupy the academy as an act of resistance. Through my journey, I realized my entry into higher education was not to find comrades, but to bring along the voices of those "who have been left out of reflection upon a society, both its past and present" (Thomas, 1998, para. 32). Higher education is a place for us to gather and constructively channel and release our anger for the past and present, not a place to rest.

If you have encountered any of the challenges I have shared throughout this chapter, please know that you are not the first or only one. Scholars will continue to address academic freedom and security and create solutions. The history of social transformation attests to the need for "coordinated efforts of multiple groups and stakeholders to collectively challenge institutional practices or policies" (Seider & Graves, 2020, p. 149). To be clear, this is not a higher education problem, it is a symptom of systemic oppression and capitalism present in all institutions and demands a mixed methods approach. In the meantime, seek a licensed mental health professional who can help you navigate, mentally and emotionally process your experiences and do not neglect your physical health. Acquire mentors from other institutions or industries who can offer suggestions and act as allies without seeking to protect the current systems of power. Last, I suggest you exercise your religion's version of prayer or spiritual meditation. In works like Bergin and Richards's (1997) "A Spiritual Strategy for Counseling and Psychotherapy," , we find spiritual strategies built on "religious practices such as prayer continue to serve as a healing intervention and motivation for survival. These practices have endured for centuries because, in different ways, they express and respond to people's deepest needs, concerns, and problems" (pp. 201–202). Through prayer and our collective reflection, we interpret experiences and understand the challenges we face to develop more practical strategies for facing future challenges. In joining in awareness and celebration of our collective existence, we can prepare our souls to receive the sound of hope that exists in the midst of what seems like chaos.

A PRAYER OF HOPE

This book raises a call to remember those who serve as adjuncts and honor the contributions made at their hands. In this chapter, I have tried to urge readers and institutions to remember and prioritize adjuncts by making intentional changes to address the patriarchal culture deeply rooted in the matrix of power that has long acknowledged and honored individuals based on the position they occupy, not their personal talents. While intentionally changing is a multiphase process of monitoring and assessment, it can be achieved (Cordeiro, 2010, p. 165). Through the brutal experiences humanity has caused, witnessed, and survived, music remains a medium that allows for us to openly grieve, celebrate, strategize, and connect with others. In the center of the Cold War, America was again confronted with the violence openly committed against African-Americans during the freedom movement most commonly referred to as the civil rights movement. Alongside a violent season of laboring and countering attempts to erase Black life, the 1950s ushered in a new wave "as eloquent African-American intellectuals and artists began to be heard as critics of segregation and as cultural innovators" (Painter, 2006, p. 256). Again, the United States saw this unveiling as an opportunity to capitalize on the artistry and knowledge

40 ▪ S. J. McKISSICK

Black Americans had acquired throughout enslavement and ongoing oppression. Nell Irvin Painter (2006) summarizes this saying,

> The U.S. State Department and the United States Information Agency (USIA) began utilizing the new post-war generation of African American in the Cold War competition with the Soviet Union. Rather than continuing to deny or cover up racial discrimination, the U.S. government began to send black artists and intellectuals on goodwill tours throughout the world. (p. 257)

This competition allowed for musical genres like jazz to spread throughout the world through the work of popular musicians like Louis Armstrong and Dizzy Gillespie. Jazz remains one of the most complex musical genres because of its use of planned sounds and spontaneity. Each musician respects the talent of their peers while freely exploring their own talent within the way they have all agreed to play a musical piece. The solo in a jazz piece allows for disruption in the midst of the fluid expression each musical piece creates and is never performed the same way twice. Likewise, higher education must practice a just-inclusion of adjuncts that reflects the prioritization of our talent and allows us security and space to freely explore the chaotic pit of knowledge and return with a vision of our future (Lorde, 2018, p. 18). This collaboration rejects the current system of controlled visibility because it is consensual and agrees to honor individual needs and differences.

Rather than being an instrument of systemic oppression that permits gender and racial capitalism, institutions should serve as a beacon of intellectual hope and advocate for academic freedom. Audre Lorde (2018) is often referenced for her comments regarding the tools of patriarchy not being able to dismantle patriarchal systems. She questions, "What does it mean when the tools of a racist patriarchy are used to examine the fruits of that same patriarchy? It means that only the most narrow perimeters of change are possible and allowable" (p. 17). It is my hope that in reading this chapter, adjuncts find the courage to continue shepherding the next generation of leaders. You are not alone. And to gatekeepers of knowledge and higher education institutions, your days are numbered. We have always known how to build spaces that celebrate our talent, stories, and existence, and we have no intention of using your tools to achieve what you believe is impossible.

REFERENCES

Bergin, A. E., & Richards, P. S. (1997). *A spiritual strategy for counseling and psychotherapy.* American Psychological Association.

Campbell, A. V. (2005). The courageous shepherd. In R. C. Dykstra (Ed.), *Images of pastoral care: Classic readings* (pp. 54–61). Chalice Press.

Cannon, K. G. (2006). *Black womanist ethics.* Wipf and Stock.

Carrero Lopez, Kyle. [@kycarrerolopez]. (2022, June 6). Academia loves to establish hierarchy with titles like 'visiting assistant just-poppin-in associate substitute non-senior junior varsity' professor most of the profs [*sic*] who really changed my life in undergrad were ones with titles like these, usually working in younger or more 'fringe' fields. Serious, generous scholars who lacked nothing other than tenure and years teaching in one place [Tweet]. Retrieved from https://twitter.com/kycarrerolopez/status/1533853339426906120?s=20&t=Xx3qgAJbD5A03l4spx6BUw.

Cordeiro, W. (2010). *Leading on empty: Refilling your tank and renewing your passion*. Baker Publishing Group.

Farmer, P. (2005). *Pathologies of power: Health, human rights, and the new war on the poor*. University of California Press.

Lorde, A. (2018). *The master's tools will never dismantle the master's house*. Penguin Books, Limited.

National Center for Education Statistics. (2016). Digest of education statistics, 2004 (NCES Publication No. 2006005). U.S. Department of Education.

Painter, N. I. (2006). *Creating Black Americans: African-American history and its meanings, 1619 to the present*. Oxford University Press.

Reichman, H. (2020, December). *Do adjuncts have academic freedom? or Why tenure matters*. American Association of University Professors. Retrieved June 23, 2022, from https://www.aaup.org/article/do-adjuncts-have-academic-freedom-or-why-tenure-matters#.YtwyxuzMK1E

Robichaud, A., & Crevier, J. (2016). Elitism and education: A critical reading of Bourdieu's theses using the work of Jürgen Habermas. *Le philosophoire*, 46, 37–58. https://www.cairn-int.info/journal-le-philosophoire-2016-2-page-37.htm

Seider, S., & Graves, D. (2020). *Schooling for critical consciousness: Engaging Black and Latinx youth in analyzing, navigating, and challenging racial injustice*. Harvard Education Press.

Sheppard, P. (2011). *Self, culture, and others in womanist practical theology*. Palgrave Macmillan US.

Taylor, J. (1998). Womanism: A methodologic framework for African American women. *Advances in Nursing Science, 21*(1), 53–64.

Thomas, L. E. (1998). Womanist theology, epistemology, and a new anthropological paradigm. *CrossCurrents, 48*(4), 488–499. http://www.jstor.org/stable/24461012

Townes, E. M., & Cannon, K. G. (2021). Foreword to the twenty-fifth anniversary edition. In *Katie's Canon: Womanism and the Soul of the Black Community* (Expanded 25th anniversary ed., pp. xvii–xx). Fortress Press.

Townsend Gilkes, C. (1997). A conscious connection to all that is. In E. M. Townes (Ed.), *Embracing the spirit: Womanist perspectives on hope, salvation, and transformation* (pp. 275–293). Orbis Books.

Walker, A. (1984). *In search of our mothers' gardens: Womanist prose*. Women's Press.

Walker, A. (2003). *The color purple*. Harcourt.

Yakoboski, P. (2018). *Adjunct faculty: Who they are and what is their experience?* TIAA Institute. Retrieved July 17, 2022, from https://www.tiaainstitute.org/sites/default/files/presentations/2018-11/TIAA_Adjunct_Faculty%20R1m%20%2010-30-18.%20FINAL.pdf

CHAPTER 4

BOTH SIDES OF THE FENCE

Danny E. Malone, Jr.

ABSTRACT

In this personal narrative, Danny describes his experiences as a tenure-track faculty member who also served as an adjunct faculty member at his former institution for 6 years—teaching both undergraduate and graduate courses year around. He explores the opportunities and challenges of being an adjunct faculty member while also relaying tips and strategies toward success for individuals interested in becoming an adjunct faculty member.

PREVIOUS ACADEMIC POSITION

My academic journey began in Fall 2016 when I started my first tenure-track position as assistant professor of sociology and criminology at then Coker College (now Coker University). What I found out quickly is, at a small private liberal arts institution, a faculty member does a lot. I taught both undergraduate and graduate courses both in-seat and online during my time at Coker, while advising students and serving on committees. Outside of my contract, I also taught as an adjunct faculty during the winter and summer terms while at Coker.

Don't Forget About the Adjuncts!, pages 43–47
Copyright © 2023 by Information Age Publishing
www.infoagepub.com
All rights of reproduction in any form reserved.

44 • D. E. MALONE, Jr.

My experiences as an adjunct faculty, in my opinion, is unique because I was also a tenure-track faculty member at the same institution. However, this positionality presented an opportunity to see the institution through the eyes of adjunct faculty, who are contracted by term, receive less compensation for the teaching load as a tenure-track faculty member, and provided less resources to teach. Moreover, it was during faculty senate meetings where I really learned about who had voting privileges and how that impacts adjunct faculty. As a sociologist, I found it interesting how status created a tenure/tenure-track faculty versus adjunct faculty tension. I want to share my insights on being both a tenure-track faculty member and adjunct faculty member at the same institution. My hope is to highlight the need to support all adjunct faculty because they are on the same team whether it is with our students or within our faculty ranks.

MY ADJUNCT FACULTY CHALLENGES

My challenges were different because I was also a tenure-track faculty member at the same institution, but nonetheless, I did note some obstacles adjunct faculty had to deal with. One thing I noted is that I did not receive any training on what it is to be an adjunct faculty member. Now, there was a 1-day orientation for new adjunct faculty members where they learned about our learning management system, resources, and teaching responsibilities. I assume I was not required to attend the session because it would be redundant. With that said, I do believe tenured/tenure-track faculty should receive invitations to these sessions because adjunct faculty are a part of the faculty, and these are opportunities for all parties to get to know one another. We all work with the same students, in the same department, at the same institution. As a full-time faculty member, I would like to know who my students' instructors are if they are including them in what the department is doing so everyone is on one accord. I cannot say that adjunct faculty were aware of department happenings. They were instructors assigned to a class and they develop the course to their liking. This does give adjunct faculty autonomy which is great because there is no template to follow regarding course material, but this can be an issue if there is no connection to overall department objectives and learning outcomes. Moreover, when course assessments are done by full-time faculty, they may not have the best data if adjunct faculty are unaware of what the department is assessing in respect to course objectives.

If I am thinking purely about adjunct faculty from the outside looking in, one of the biggest issues would be office space. As a faculty member with teaching responsibilities, students should have an office space where they can meet with any teaching faculty where they can have privacy. What I noted from seeing some of the adjunct faculty is that they met with students in the library or other public access spaces. While an adjunct faculty member could get a room in the library to meet, this is not always an option as students use those rooms to study. Institutional leadership should invest in a physical space where adjunct faculty can prepare for their lectures and meet with students and others.

A very big challenge for adjunct faculty is compensation. Now this varies by institution, but for all of the work that goes into designing a course, creating assignments, grading assignments, and meeting with students, adjunct faculty are severely underpaid. As higher education continues to tighten its belt and tenure-track positions are not coming up as often, we will see more adjunct faculty position appear but the compensation may not be worth it. Adjunct faculty, more broadly contingent faculty, occupy about 73% faculty position in higher education (American Association of University Professors, 2018). This is the silenced majority, and I say that because their voices are marginalized in higher education. For this group, they are term-to-term or year-to-year and if they "ruffle feathers" like speak out against inequities and express ideas in class that students may push back against, they may jeopardize their future employment. Moreover, their work conditions can effect student learning conditions because if their contract renewal is tenuous and dependent upon student approval and conditioned by a lack of academic freedom, then adjunct faculty are between a rock and a hard place. I find this challenge to be the deepest because higher education depends heavily on adjunct faculty but treats them like cogs in a machine. If adjunct faculty do not have institutional support that would increase student success, then we do not allow them to fulfill the academic duties of faculty which is to challenge our students to think outside of the box—to question "taken-for-granted" assumptions. Ultimately, we have cheapened the value of higher education because adjunct faculty are hamstrung by lack of protections and academia has devalued the adjunct faculty position. I believe tenured/tenure-track faculty should do more to get their leadership to provide decent protections for adjunct faculty. Leadership should recognize the role adjunct faculty play in keeping their institutions afloat.

MY ADJUNCT FACULTY OPPORTUNITIES

Just as my challenges are different, my opportunities are also different. As an adjunct faculty member, I saw that sometimes full-time faculty members take what they have for granted. For instance, having an office to meet students. For adjunct faculty, finding creative ways to meet and engage with students

46 • D. E. MALONE, Jr.

presents an opportunity to stand out with students. Students may not always know the difference between adjunct faculty and full-time faculty, but they will always know who showed up for them. For example, when students have events on campus and you have time, show up and cheer them on. I did see adjunct faculty members at sporting events at my former institution and the students did thank them for making time to cheer them on.

TIPS AND STRATEGIES FOR ADJUNCT FACULTY

I do feel it is important to find ways to integrate into the campus life. This means volunteering time with student organizations, meeting with full-time faculty from time to time, and asking administrators if you can be an asset in any way outside of teaching. If you are already doing these things, please keep a working document of them and keep your immediate supervisors in the loop. One thing about higher education is, it revolves around students. So as an adjunct faculty member, if you can get students to buy into you, then you have a good chance to leverage that into other opportunities.

Another tip I would give to any person interested in adjunct teaching is if you are an academic, please continue to publish. I know it is tough but it is about staying relevant in the field. You can teach great all day but if you want to stand out for many of these institutions that have a lot of adjunct faculty applying, they want to see that you are an active scholar. Publishing may not be required for promotion or tenure, but publishing can lead to greater opportunities because you are going above and beyond. Primarily, this is just one way to separate yourself from the crowd. So for example, if you are at a community college and publishing, if you want to try to move to a private liberal arts institution then you may be asked for an interview based on the mere fact that not only are you a good teacher, but you are active in your field even when your job does not require it. Me personally, I do more than what is required because I am confident it will lead to greater opportunities. Even if you are not thinking of leaving, publishing and gaining public notoriety will get the attention of your supervisor. This may encourage them to find ways to keep you so be sure you are sending them an updated CV every so often. I believe adjunct faculty should send their CVs to their supervisors so the institution can review their talents to see if there are opportunities where the adjunct faculty can add more value to the institution. I believe this practice also communicates that the adjunct faculty member sees value in themselves and the institution they are employed with. Lastly, this should be standard practice for adjunct faculty, so they are consistently aware of how they are progressing in their career.

SHOW UP AND BE PRESENT

No matter my role, as a tenure-track faculty or an adjunct faculty member, I show up and am present. It is a pride thing for me because whatever I do reflects who I am, what I represent, and how I feel about my job. There will always be people who are negative and project their insecurities onto you but you should do your best to avoid those individuals. Your responsibility is to be present in the classroom for students and complete tasks associated with your job. Engaging with students whether it is in person, email, or through video chats, I am present to be sure they are in a position to be successful. You do not have to be a tenure/tenure-track faculty member for this to happen. You just have to be a faculty member who is willing to show up and be present at your institution.

LAST WORDS

What I want readers to take away from my experience is that I respect adjunct (more broadly contingent) faculty and feel higher education would crumble if adjunct faculty were not present. Being an adjunct faculty member is not for the faint of heart as the workloads are heavy and the compensation is low. There are challenges and opportunities that come with an adjunct faculty that I believe tenure/tenure-track faculty don't always take into account. Also, I do feel that tenure/tenure-track faculty should do more to bring adjunct faculty into the fold regarding department matters as we all are working towards helping our students succeed. At the same time, there are tenure/tenure-track faculty who will advocate for you as I have advocated for voting rights for adjunct faculty at my previous institution. I encourage adjunct faculty to stay encouraged, love what you do, make the most of the opportunities, and know that you matter in higher education.

REFERENCE

American Association of University Professors. (2018). *Data snapshot: Contingent faculty in US higher ed.* https://www.aaup.org/file/10112018%20Data%20Snapshot%20Tenure.pdf

PART II

THE VALUE OF CONTINUOUS IMPROVEMENT

CHAPTER 5

IMPROVING THE INSTRUCTIONAL SKILLS OF ADJUNCT FACULTY THROUGH PROFESSIONAL DEVELOPMENT

Ramycia McGhee

ABSTRACT

Adjunct faculty are vital to higher education, comprising over one-half of all faculty members in the United States. Campuses relying heavily on adjunct faculty must understand that proper support is needed so these valuable staff members may continue to become proficient instructors. In order to create and maintain an effective adjunct workforce, administrators in higher education must support the needs of adjunct faculty members. The purpose of this chapter is to highlight challenges adjuncts face in higher education while emphasizing opportunities created for adjunct faculty, and providing tools, tips, and strategies for current and potential adjunct faculty. Lastly, this chapter underscores affirmations to assist in the promotion of adjunct faculty members' self-efficacy.

Don't Forget About the Adjuncts!, pages 51–61
Copyright © 2023 by Information Age Publishing
www.infoagepub.com
All rights of reproduction in any form reserved.

DEFINITION OF TERMS

Adjunct faculty: Teachers and professors who are employed on a contract per term or per course; also part-time faculty (Bergmann, 2011).

Part-time faculty. The characteristics of part-time faculty are they are less likely to be White, less likely to have a terminal degree, they make less total money than full-time faculty, and are significantly more likely to have another full-time job someplace else (Monks, 2009).

Full-time faculty. Teachers and professors who are permanently employed full-time by the institution (Bergmann, 2011).

OVERVIEW OF PREVIOUS AND CURRENT ADJUNCT POSITIONS HELD WITHIN HIGHER EDUCATION

Although my employment for the past 5½ years has been as a full-time tenured faculty, this was not always the case due to serving as an adjunct professor for 8 years at various institutions in the Midwest. The courses I taught were developmental English, which introduced students to the process of academic reading, writing, discourse, various writing techniques, and sentence and paragraph structures. I also taught English credit courses, which emphasized the importance of the writing process, purpose and audience, organization, mechanics, and critical reading and thinking. In teaching research writing courses, I was able to assist students in honing in on their research methodologies, peer review, and the production of a quality research paper.

My responsibilities as an adjunct were to teach three, 3-credit courses per the adjunct contract. Teaching those courses involved: planning and creating lectures; facilitating in-class discussions; assigning projects; and grading papers, quizzes, and exams. In addition, my other duties involved assessing grades for students based on participation, in-class performance, assignments, and examinations. Lastly, I reported student learning outcomes and participated in class reviews conducted by the department's adjunct coordinator.

CHALLENGES

Serving as an adjunct instructor caused me to face many challenges, including: financial instability, lack of professional development opportunities provided by the college and or department, being seen as "equal" by full-time tenured faculty, lack of promotional/advancement opportunities, and unsolicited mentorship.

Financial Instability

According to Inside Higher Ed, Eric Farwell (2020) states, "Recently, it's come to the public's attention that adjuncts often make $25,000 or less during any given year, which is below the poverty line for a family of four" (para. 4). Many adjuncts face the uncertainty of stable academic employment, and this was definitely my situation. The summer months in particular were extremely hard, due to the lack of available courses offered. Oftentimes, tenured faculty would teach the bulk of the classes offered, thus leaving me to explore teaching opportunities at other colleges within the district, but the same situation ensued. Therefore, I was often left without employment during the summer months after receiving marginal pay during the school year. Thus, I was extremely frustrated and sometimes was not able to enjoy my summer break, due to constantly looking for ways to earn income.

Lack of Professional Development Opportunities

The professional development offered by the department and or college for adjunct faculty was few and far in between, and often unpaid. Moreover, adjunct professors were not at the helm of the professional development creation, which resulted from adjunct faculty being undervalued. Farwell (2020) states, "More money would be nice, but so would practical workshops, networking events and mentoring that could help adjuncts..." (para. 6). Hence, while increasing adjuncts' pay would be phenomenal, however, because that seems to not be the priority, perhaps increasing conferencing opportunities, and other professional development prospects would be more pragmatic. Moreover, considering adjunct faculty were often not a part of the planning process of said professional development opportunities, these opportunities often were during the times that full-time faculty and administrators were available. Therefore, when professional development opportunities were offered it was during times I was unavailable due to prior obligations such as working a second job, teaching and preparing for classes. Also, alternative times and locations for professional development were usually unavailable. Thus, I was often faced with the choice between: sharpening my teaching skills and bonding with other teaching faculty (both full-time and part-time), securing additional hours from my second job, making time to become fully prepared for my students, or completing my own doctoral studies. This was extremely disappointing considering professional development is essential and has many advantages for adjunct faculty, such as the enhancement of one's curriculum *vitae*, learning new teaching skills and methodologies, receiving coaching opportunities, and enjoying a sense of faculty camaraderie.

Not Being Seen as an Equal Colleague

In my experience, it often felt like many full-time tenured faculty members did not view me as an equal colleague, and there appeared to be subtle bias against me as a part-time faculty member. This could be due to my limited teaching load as an adjunct, as well as my teaching at multiple institutions in and outside of the district. Thus, it seemed that full-timers often felt that as an adjunct, I had no "real" investment in the institution, department, and or student body. Some tenured faculty also believed as an adjunct faculty, I did not produce or publish scholarly work. According to Inside Higher Ed, Angela B. Fulk (2019) states, "If we are willing to work under the low-wage, low-respect conditions the college offers, we are by definition complicit in our own exploitation" (para. 14). However, I often told full-time tenured faculty they failed to realize that many of us adjunct faculty are accepting these conditions due to our belief that we are making an investment towards one day securing a full-time tenured track position either at our current institution or someplace else.

Lack of Promotional/Advancement Opportunities

Due to various factors, the lack of promotional/advancement opportunities was slim. If full-time tenured track positions became available within the institution or the district, I definitely applied. If other academically centered positions became available, I also applied for those opportunities. However, in my department, the same tenured faculty were selected to be on the hiring committee each time which would make it difficult for other (more valuing of adjuncts) tenured faculty to be on the committee or a part of the selection process. This resulted in a lack of diversity in candidate selection. Through the rumor mill, it was often said that the committee "cherry-picked" their candidates, while reviewing other candidates only for formality purposes. A common practice in my department was that, if the committee decided to hire from the adjunct pool in the department, they always selected individuals who looked, acted, and thought like them. Basically, they were hiring mirror images of themselves, leaving no room for academic or racial equity, diversity, or inclusion. Thus, the department landscape was "stunted," and growth remained limited for potential promotional prospects. This of course frustrated me with the department, and as a way of navigating this situation, I continued to apply regardless of who was on the committee and not just at my institution or district but all over. Also, I began to make connections with various individuals by volunteering to substitute classes, attending department meetings, and often taking advantage of serving on district-level ad hoc committee(s) when they were available. This was all in an effort to become more visible on campus while keeping a pulse on who was doing what, and which conversations were being had. I had to learn who I could (or would) potentially be interviewing with, while investigating who may be planning or even considering serving on the hiring committee.

Unsolicited Mentorship

While mentorship is greatly needed and wanted, there is a way it should be done to be productive and meaningful. Unfortunately, that was not the case for me as an adjunct professor. The attempted mentorship I received was often counterproductive. Firstly, I believe mentees should have the opportunity to choose their mentors, not the other way around. There were several instances where women in higher education tried to appoint themselves as my mentor without my consent. They did not attempt to have a conversation with me about being my potential mentor and instead deemed themselves my mentor during meetings, lunches, and even via email. They attempted to force me into one particular career direction while trying to manipulate me by using their position within the institution to influence my professional decisions. Lastly, these self-appointed mentors, oftentimes looked like me and we shared the same ethnic and cultural backgrounds, they were just much older and had been in academia much longer. They tried to convey to me that I needed to dress, act, and communicate a certain way (amongst other things) to move up in the institution or in higher education in general. Due to their abrasiveness, this made me very uneasy and I found it quite disturbing. It felt more like academic "hazing," which is a form of academic bullying, that in itself is extremely harmful and I knew I couldn't thrive in working with any of them on any level. Only 23 years old (and looking younger) when I started adjuncting, they likely felt I needed and wanted guidance. While that may have been the case, their approach did not seem mutual or professional—it felt more parental and uninvited. Hence, it was not received well. I didn't need parents at work. Rather, I needed colleagues, healthy mentors, and career coaches. Unfortunately, I was receiving none of those things from these self-appointed mentors.

OPPORTUNITIES

Being an adjunct created several opportunities for me such as providing me with ample teaching experience; constructing my teaching philosophy; identifying a healthy mentor; seeking professional development prospects in and outside the institution; and lastly, allotting me flexibility.

Teaching Experience

As an adjunct, I was able to gain an immense amount of teaching experience while teaching a variety of classes from developmental to advanced courses. Such as developmental writing which underscored the fundamentals of academic college writing; research writing courses that emphasized the importance of research methodologies, evaluating credible sources, and lastly, the elements and caliber of an academic research paper.

This experience enabled me to: learn and implement classroom management techniques, build student relationships while implementing appropriate boundaries, and understand the importance of being nimble and savvy in and out of the classroom. Moreover, I was able to teach at multiple institutions, which afforded me the opportunity of learning how different colleges and departments are run, student bodies operate, and various cultures exist within one district. Additionally, I was able to continuously improve my teaching andragogy and, most importantly, gain confidence in my teaching ability. Being secure in my teaching abilities permitted me the luxury of creating solid and engaging teaching materials, as well as producing quality teaching demonstrations while on the job market. In fact, I believe that because my teaching demonstrations were so diverse, inclusive, interactive, and efficient, I was able to advance through interview processes, and subsequently, be offered my current position.

Teaching Philosophy Development

My adjunct experiences helped me create my philosophy on teaching, and as a result, it allowed me to develop and modify my teaching materials and develop my students. Consequently, being an adjunct helped me understand what kind of teacher I wanted to be. Moreover, on the job market, analyzing a teaching philosophy is an essential part of learning about a potential candidate. Hence, the formulation of my teaching philosophy demonstrated my willingness to reflect, and pivot in response to the feedback from my students, as well as communicate my future short and long-term goals in academia. These skills are essential, as they keep me grounded in my teaching approach, encourage me to reflect on my career goals and aspirations while keeping my students' needs at the forefront of my mind. All in all, my teaching philosophy is a constant reminder of the professor I am and will continue to be.

Identify a Healthy Mentor

Knowing what I did not want in a mentor, helped me to pinpoint what I wanted and needed in a mentor. With that being said, I was able to cultivate a relationship with a female tenured faculty member on my own terms. This relationship was genuine, gentle, and rooted in love. We were able to bond over many things outside of work, which made it really easy to discuss career plans, goals, aspirations, and even personal things. She constantly encouraged me and presented opportunities to me just by asking if I wanted to be a part of things happening in the college and department. While on the job market, she assisted me in strengthening my application materials, and when I didn't get offered positions, she provided reassurance, support, and encouragement. We formed such a great relationship, that when I was offered my full-time position, she was ecstatic and sat down with me to review my new job contract, while discussing what they should be offering me regarding compensation. To this day, we still keep in touch regularly, and I keep her abreast of all my professional accolades and personal triumphs. She is always so proud, gracious, and loving—embodying what a mentor should be and as a bonus, she shares my racial and ethnic background.

Identify Professional Development Opportunities Outside of the Institution

Due to limited professional development opportunities being offered by my former institution, I was able to conduct research and be a part of professional development opportunities outside of my college. This allotted me the chance to network and build relationships with other adjunct and tenured faculty as well as administrators at other colleges. I was able to build my curriculum vitae by attending various professional development opportunities that not only centered higher education but academia as a whole. As a result of attending these training and professional development opportunities, I was able to incorporate additional tools, tips, and strategies in my classroom, in addition to sharpening my expertise as a scholar.

Flexibility

One of the major benefits of being an adjunct was the flexibility it provided. I was able to customize my schedule while budgeting my time and money. As a result, I was able to complete my doctoral studies and create an action research project which resulted in my dissertation's focus. Henceforth, my dissertation was focused on the professional development of adjunct faculty resulting in my creation of an online training program to assist adjunct faculty in improving their instructional skills (McGhee, 2015).

TIPS/STRATEGIES FOR OTHER CURRENT AND POTENTIAL ADJUNCT FACULTY ENTERING THE FIELD

Focus on Your Andragogy

Since teaching is the most important skill of the job, it is crucial that potential adjuncts hone their teaching abilities and sharpen their skill sets. There are a number of ways to do this. First, teach a variety of classes in your department ranging from introductory courses to advanced courses. Second, teach at other institutions—although the classes may not be exactly the same, it allows you to refresh and modify your teaching material, so it aligns with the culture of the classroom. Third, identify professional development opportunities provided by your current institution as well as those that are not. Be sure these professional development opportunities are: centered on teaching methodologies, stay on the cutting edge of the discipline you are teaching in, and allow you to stay abreast of conferences that involve andragogy and pedagogy. Last, identify individuals who are teaching the same or similar courses in an effort to build coalitions and develop a network to share teaching methodologies and ideas.

Develop Healthy Student–Professor Relationships

Formulating appropriate student relationships as a professor is very special. It shows the students you care for them, their well-being, and their development as a scholar moving through to the next level in their pursuit of higher education. Moreover, it makes your job as an instructor easier because you have developed a strong rapport, and students gravitate toward genuine, trustworthy faculty. Essentially, they feel safe to: confide in you; ask for letters and recommendations; and participate in class and ask questions. Overall, they will feel comfortable to continue building a relationship with you when they leave your class and keep you abreast of their academic and personal achievements. These things are important because they are "fruits" of your labor, they are success stories, lastly, they are living breathing narratives and can, and often do serve as testimonies to your teaching abilities.

Identify a Healthy Mentor(s)

Identifying a mentor is crucial in all parts of life, and academia is no exception. Although this may present a challenge, it will be worth it in the end. I recommend identifying a more seasoned faculty member who you can connect with and have a professional relationship. A way to "break the ice" would just be to speak and strike up a "small talk" conversation about how their term or semester is going, how many students they have, do they have any favorite students or challenging students, and so on. Nevertheless, if you are uncomfortable with this approach, perhaps you might email them to ask if it would be ok to audit one of their classes as you are trying to sharpen your teaching skills and are curious to know how they cover certain topics in their class. Above all be yourself and be natural, you will know when you have found your mentor. Moreover, by identifying your mentor, they could assist you in receiving feedback on your teaching methodologies as well as possibly introduce you to new ones, aid you in carving out your career path, and be a sounding board for challenges you may face as an adjunct faculty or a teaching faculty in general. Furthermore, you will have a connection with someone who can give you more information about the department and institution as a whole, as well as higher education in general.

Learn and Embrace Your Value

Although you are an adjunct faculty member, remember you are not less than "adjuncts making up 40 to 75 percent of faculty instructors at any given college and university" (Farwell, 2020, para. 4). Therefore, there is a huge dependency placed on adjunct faculty. Thus, you are invaluable to an extent and can use that to your advantage. Due to this, understand you do not have to agree to every "opportunity" you are presented with at your institution. Feel free to volunteer for things you see of value to your growth and development as a faculty member, and don't be afraid to say, "No" (Tomlin, 2022). Do not be afraid to customize your teaching schedule to do other things with your time, out of fear you will not receive any classes. Do not be afraid to attend the departmental meeting, so you have firsthand knowledge of what is going on in the department and can even voice your concern(s).

Apply Apply Apply

Be open to applying for similar positions within academia. These positions could be coordinator positions, tutoring assignments, associate dean positions, dean positions, and so on. These positions, although not directly related to teaching, can still be used as an opportunity for learning additional information regarding higher education. Be empowered to apply for career opportunities outside of your home state. This helps to broaden additional job prospects and career advancement opportunities. Thus, this

60 • R. McGHEE

could be an opportunity to use all the skills and training gained over your adjunct teaching years as a way to secure a full-time tenured track teaching position if one desires.

Affirmations

I have three affirmations that spoke, and continue to speak, to me.

1. "It won't always be like this"—kept me going: Everything is temporary, and things do change.
2. "The money will come." This affirmation came from my mentor, which allowed me to review opportunities for career-building versus monetary compensation.
3. "Things don't happen to me, they happen for me." This affirmation permits me to reexamine circumstances through a different lens.
4. "Success is a journey, not a destination—Keep moving forward!"—This is an affirmation I always keep in mind, which reminds me I am a lifelong learner and I am still on assignment. This is in the signature of my email.

CONCLUSION

Readers take away several things from this chapter such as being open to being a lifelong learner. This is imperative because it allows you to constantly be open to gaining new knowledge, learning new experiences, and executing new tasks. Next, put personal and professional development at the forefront of your mind. Remember, to think of each opportunity as a notch on your CV, a way to better increase your chances of obtaining a full-time position, whether in academia or industry. Lastly, embracing the adjunct journey is rewarding, in that it allows you to watch and be a part of your student's academic, professional, and personal journeys. Overall, being an adjunct is satisfying work!

REFERENCES

Bergmann, D. (2011). *A study of adjunct faculty* [Unpublished Doctoral dissertation]. Montana State University. https://scholarworks.montana.edu/xmlui/bitstream/handle/1/911/BergmannD0811.pdf?sequence=1&isAllowed=y

Farwell, E. (2020, October 7). *It's time to give adjuncts more professional opportunities.* https://www.insidehighered.com/views/2020/10/07/its-time-offer-professional-development-opportunities-adjuncts-opinion

Fulk, B. A. (2019, February 14). *Confronting biases against adjunct faculty.* https://www.insidehighered.com/advice/2019/02/14/how-bias-toward-adjuncts-plays-out-among-students-other-faculty-and-administrators

McGhee, R. (2015). *Improving the instructional skills of adjunct faculty through professional development: An action research study* [Unpublished doctoral dissertation]. Capella University. https://www.proquest.com/openview/2420d60eb5123e385daa4c620aa92ca7/1?pq-origsite=gscholar&cbl=18750

Monks, J. (2009). *Who are the part-time faculty? There's no such thing as a typical part-timer.* American Association of University Professors. https://www.aaup.org/article/who-are-part-time-faculty#.YridTXbML.rf

Tomlin, A. D. (2022). *I'm a Black PhD, and I still have to fight!* In A. M. Allen & J. T. Stewart (Eds.), *We're not OK: Black faculty experiences and higher education strategies* (pp. 58–74). Cambridge University Press.

CHAPTER 6

TO BE AN AFRICAN CENTERED EDUCATOR IN 21ST CENTURY SOCIAL WORK EDUCATION

Senemeht Olatunji

ABSTRACT

Research has increased regarding the infusion of African centered social work practice principles into the profession (Bent-Goodley et al., 2017) as a means to resist domination and oppression and support liberation for people of the African diaspora (Akbar, 1984). Growing up in an African-centered spiritual practice has informed my almost 2 decades as an educator in both secondary and postsecondary settings. As an adjunct professor in New York, I have spent the past 4 years utilizing African centered values to promote efficacious academic experiences. Students often remark that despite the cultural diversity of New York City, I am often their first Black, female professor. Utilizing African centered practices creates an academic environment rooted in empathy and centered on healing. Inculcating African centered practices and modalities into the classroom and interactions with students, often alleviates many of the additional challenges that come with the role of adjunct.

Don't Forget About the Adjuncts!, pages 63–71
Copyright © 2023 by Information Age Publishing
www.infoagepub.com
All rights of reproduction in any form reserved.

FINDING MY WAY

For the African teacher, teaching is a calling, a constant journey towards mastery,
a scientific activity, a matter of community membership, an aspect of a learning
community, a process of "becoming a library," a matter of care and custody for our
culture and traditions, a matter of a critical viewing of the wider world, and a
response to the imperative of MAAT.

—Asa Hilliard

I have spent the past 17 years as an educator and social worker and have seen firsthand how education can be a great equalizer for those society has marginalized. In my roles, I have created inclusive environments for all the youth and adults I have worked with, celebrated their diverse needs and backgrounds, and passionately pursued equitable access to everything our society has to offer. My journey here was mapped out long before it started. In high school, my English teacher wrote a letter of recommendation for my college applications. In the letter, she stated, "Senemeht is a defender of the underdog and works to dismantle injustices both large and small." At the time, I did not know that this innate trait would one day be catalytic for my path to social work. My own journey began in an Introduction to social work course as a junior at Marymount Manhattan College. My then professor challenged us to look beyond our biases and value judgments, challenging us to see the world through the lens of those we would serve. She encouraged critical thought and dialogue and expected us to challenge our worldviews that were limited in scope and perpetuated systems of oppression. At the time I did not know I would eventually pursue a career in social work, but this class forced me to grow in ways I did not imagine a class could. I remember having an aha moment, thinking that education should leave you feeling stretched and challenged. If you leave a class thinking and doing the same way you entered, that is a profound loss.

I started in the classroom as a high school English teacher in Washington, DC. The classroom has always been a way to bring ideas alive and integrate students' lived experiences with concepts they will learn. My career took me to various avenues in education before pursuing my Master of Social Work at Howard University. After 6 years of experience working as a secondary educator and instructional coach and practice experience in mental health treatment, domestic violence and sexual assault, transitional housing and homelessness, and child welfare, my journey eventually led me back to the classroom.

In January 2018, I began as adjunct faculty at the Silberman School of Social Work at Hunter College in New York City and was appointed to teach Introduction to Social Work, a gateway course for students interested in social work but unsure if the profession was their pathway. It was critical for me that students have an exemplary grounding in the foundation of social work, both the positive and negative. A year into my tenure, Social Welfare Policy was added to my course load. I have long had an interest in policy and the way in which it shapes and influences the lives of those we serve. It was a wonderful challenge for students to enter the classroom with assumptions about policy and feelings of the subject matter being boring. I used this opportunity to break down policy in a way that was understandable and engaging. In 2021, I decided that I wanted to take a sabbatical from teaching. While I love teaching, I knew I needed a break. I was then asked to teach Social Welfare Policy II: Child Welfare, a course I have wanted to teach for several years. I could not pass on the opportunity to teach a field of practice that I am passionate about. I spent 4 years as a social worker in the child welfare system in the District of Columbia working primarily with youth transitioning out of the system. Additionally, my last position was as a director of a college preparatory program for youth in foster care in New York. These roles provided me with practice wisdom and expertise on issues that directly impact youth in the foster care system. Having the opportunity to teach students before they worked in a foster care setting has been a rewarding experience.

FINDING THE SOLUTION IN THE CHALLENGE

A year into teaching at Hunter, a Black female student announced to the class that I was her first Black, female professor. This revelation shocked both me and her fellow classmates. Being in New York City and in the City University of New York system, it was not lost on the class that despite being in the most diverse city, the underrepresentation of Black female faculty is still prevalent. This has created both a blessing and a challenge. For many students, when they walk into the classroom and see me, they are affirmed. While this affirmation is one that I find to be important, it often caused me to have an overwhelming number of students who vied for my attention. Students wanted to often stay after class and talk about life issues, sought guidance and counseling about challenges they were facing, needed additional help with their assignments, and often needed letters of recommendation because I was the only faculty they had a relationship with. In isolation, I had no issues with any of these things, but when you have course loads of up to 70 students and no place at the university, these demands on time often occurred after hours. While I knew my connections with students would bring the additional need for support, I was not prepared for how significant this was. Balancing these demands became key to maintaining the position.

Another challenge I found was students' increasing mental health needs. I often use the classroom to normalize mental health challenges and encourage students to seek mental wellness through appropriate therapeutic channels. Even prior to the pandemic, students had a hard time coping with the challenges in their own lives and how to balance them as full and part-time students. Many of them faced food and housing insecurity and had to choose family or work responsibilities over coming to class, or could not afford to purchase the fare to even get to class. These dynamics often caused students to experience crises and have to make the decision to leave altogether. I continue to emphasize self-care and wellness to students, and yet I am aware that without structural change, these issues will continue to persist.

AN OPPORTUNITY TO LEARN THE AFRICAN CENTERED WAY

African teachers place a premium on bringing their students into a knowledge of themselves and a knowledge of their communities. African people place great value on WHO each person is, on WHO the community is . . .

—Asa Hilliard

What is most critical in my approach to teaching is bringing an African centered viewpoint to both the content I teach and how I interact with students. I was born and raised in New York to parents who formally adopted an African centered way of living which thus shaped my worldview and who I am as a social worker and educator. Throughout my career I have used universal principles that are African centered with much success. Due to the universal nature of these principles, they have resonated with students and clients alike. To best sum up these principles I try to demonstrate through my behavior and action through the following:

> Meet life's challenges with peace; find a unified support network; always go with the win–win solution; be relentless in your pursuit of a fulfilled destiny; have an understanding that we are all interconnected; have compassion towards those who need it; always stand out as a leader and do what is correct even when no one is watching; let your speech and visualizations be reflective of success and optimism; and be ever vigilant about what you feed your mind, body and spirit.

As a practitioner, I rely heavily on African centered social work as a way to teach and serve. Founded formally as Afrocentricity by Molefi Kete Asante (1980) this theory explains the experiences of individuals of African descent across the globe. African-centered theory is attentive to the unique and collective experiences of cultures and the need to honor and validate historical and cultural identities, traits, norms, values, and symbols that can be used to empower people of African descent (Asante, 1980). Accordingly, within the field of social work, it is proposed that social workers should tailor their practices based on the cultural values and norms of the populations that they seek to serve and even more importantly, develop practice models that work with these populations (Schiele, 1996). Specifically, it was founded as a theory to understand how to provide culturally based services to individuals of the African diaspora by integrating concepts and tenets of African American culture with traditional African culture (Schiele, 1996). This is the case for education for which Afrocentric theorists argued that if students learned their African ancestral history, they might be more inclined to academically engage and perform well in school (Schiele, 1996). Using this approach helps to inculcate the universal values in students, helps them to connect cultural values to those they work with and establishes an environment of excellence in the classroom and practice.

Teaching foundational and policy-related courses in social work has provided opportunities to not only culturally affirm the students but allow them to see the people who they will work with and interact with in a culturally affirming way. Oftentimes, social work students enter the field and find that their personal values don't always align with those they will work with. This is also the case when there are cultural differences. It has been critically important to impress upon students the importance of learning about their clients through the lens of their cultural experiences. By doing so, it allows students to address their own biases and value judgments and learn from those they are working with. This alignment not only builds trust and rapport but builds the worldview of the social work student. Additionally, as they come into who they are as individuals and future practitioners, there is an awareness that has been established that this work should always be done in an efficacious way. A core principle of wanting for others, as you want for yourself is one that I often express to students. Leading with empathy and trying to understand how someone came to be in a position of need and the vulnerability it takes to ask for assistance is one that should be handled with the most care. As future social workers, I remind students that they are tasked with being a part of how the destiny of another will go and that responsibility is the greatest one could ever be tasked with. Helping students to understand the interconnectedness of the lives of those we work with, and the web of support allows them to approach learning in a way that puts accountability at the center. Establishing accountability as central to the learner is important because it establishes a way of behavior both in the classroom and in the field working with clients. When a student is accountable, they are likely to be efficacious; they will do their best in their academic coursework as well as act with the highest integrity in their field. As faculty, I take the position of role model very seriously; what I expect from my students, I expect from myself.

68 ▪ S. OLATUNJI

Another opportunity teaching allows is helping students to develop their critical thinking and ability to be solution-oriented. Embedding culture in the curriculum has an unlikely effect. It is emphasized as a means of restoring well-being for the students as well. This approach supports social work students with their own healing as well, builds empathy within students, and encourages students to imagine and dream, so as to foster hopefulness and optimism in their ability to effect change. Additionally, it builds critical reflection to take loving actions towards making a change towards policies, practices, and political decisions that may harm those they will encounter. This makes the students aware and empowers them, encouraging them to advocate for themselves and others.

My courses focus on issues related to race and ethnicity, gender, sexuality, mental health, and poverty. My teaching philosophy is rooted in an asset-based community development approach; I see my students as the underutilized assets of the university community, highlighting skills that already exist. Students are guided to bring diversity of thought, their authentic worldviews and experiences, unique cultural experiences, and innovative scholarship to find solutions to many of the grand challenges mobilizing the profession. My experience as an adjunct professor has afforded me the opportunity to learn from and understand the complex needs of students in a college setting and provide them opportunities to make systemic changes.

Every semester my students participate in a policy and program hackathon. The students are expected to actively share their ideas about social work-relevant issues that pertain to college students' experience with mental health and poverty. Students pitch their ideas within small groups, and subsequently, merge the ideas into hypothetical scenarios of the future to address or eliminate poverty or enhance mental health services on a college campus. This year we expanded the hackathon to address pandemic-related issues that are uniquely impacting higher education institutions. Every semester I host a guest lecture series with social workers across the United States for students in the Introduction to Social Work and Policy courses to expose them to various fields of practice. Students learn from social workers in both traditional and nontraditional settings, including opportunities such as the growing demand for clinicians in the National Football League (NFL). The hackathon and lecture series alike, allow students to see themselves in a multitude of settings and to find a niche where they can make a change

NAVIGATING YOUR WAY

As I culminate my journey at the Silberman School of Social Work after 4 years of teaching, I am reflective on this journey and all that it has taught me. From my experience and expertise, here are the tips and strategies I offer:

To Be an African Centered Educator in 21st Century Social Work Education • **69**

- Find a mentor who is a lifeline and connection to the university: Dr. Patricia Dempsey, the dean of the BSW program guided me through this journey and was a champion of my ability to teach on the collegiate level. She trusted me to bring quality education to the students and gave me opportunities to teach courses where I expressed interest and passion.
- Build relationships with the students outside of just teaching: It is important to get to know your students. Really understand your students, their experiences, and what they value. It allows you to understand who they are at their core and bring empathy to the classroom.
- Build relationships with your colleagues, especially those who are also adjuncts: having a community of others who understand exactly what you are experiencing is critical to maintaining balance. This tribe of colleagues will be your sounding board when teaching presents challenges and opportunities.
- Lastly, have fun! Teaching is an honor and should be the gateway to innovation and change. Trust yourself and your students to build a reciprocal relationship where learning is an exchange.

AFFIRMATIONS OF MANIFESTATION

Teaching is not always easy, and I find that affirmations that are grounding and connect me back to my purpose are critical to maintaining balance. I have several that I consistently use and are stored in my journal. I often go back to these during times of reflection and when I need answers that can only be found by going within. This is especially the case when the demands of teaching get overwhelming. I find that when I reflect on the challenges I am facing through these affirmations, it is a reminder that I influence the direction of my life through my relationship with a higher power. Teaching is an important part of my life and allows me to connect to my spirituality in a deeper way. In African-centered traditions, teaching is a sacred calling, and to be one is profoundly important. While I have many affirmations, the few I chose for the sake of this chapter are:

Affirmation 1

Infinite spirit opens the way for the divine design of my life to manifest. Let the genius in me now be released. Let me see clearly the perfect plan for wealth, health, love, and perfect expression. In the divine mind, there is only completion. Therefore, my demonstration is completed. My perfect work, my perfect home, my perfect health, my perfect love under grace in a perfect way. I give thanks that I already received on the invisible and make active preparation for receiving on the visible.

Affirmation 2

I embrace the beginnings that are unfolding. I am open to the miracles that are coming. My dreams and desires manifest. All that I wish for flows to me. I am blessed. I am loved. I am whole.

Affirmation 3

I create my own reality. I am a powerful manifestor. I shape the life that I desire. I honor my intuition. I listen to my own inner guidance. I follow the compass of my heart. I am supported fully by the universe.

I learned about these affirmations from my love of learning about astrology. I often watch videos on YouTube about the astrological influence on our lives and how we manifest our passions and desires. The affirmations I shared are among the many I have collected over the years and use in all areas of my life. These affirmations are important to me because one core belief of African centered practice is the idea that everything you need in life is already inherent within you. I am a firm believer that we all have the ability to tap into ourselves for the answers to our greatest challenges. I want students to acknowledge that while there are ever present external challenges, the answer also lies within and can be manifested outwardly.

CONCLUSION

The biggest takeaway I hope readers take from this chapter is seeing themselves in these words. We triumph when we are able to see the ways in which we are alike rather than different. Each of us has a unique story and still we face similar challenges and opportunities. Don't be discouraged and know that academia needs us to continue to pass the torch. Keep lighting the fire by way of radical, innovative, and empathic teaching. Learn from your students and show them that they don't have to wait until they have a diploma in hand to make a change.

REFERENCES

Akbar, N. (1984). Africentric social sciences for human liberation. *Journal of Black Studies, 14*(4), 395–414. https://doi.org/10.1177/002193478401400401

Asante, M. K. (1980). *Afrocentricity: The theory of social change.* Amulefi Publishing Co.

Bent-Goodley, T., Fairfax, C. N., & Carlton-LaNey, I. (2017). The significance of African-centered social work for social work practice. *Journal of Human Behavior in the Social Environment, 27*(1–2), 1–6. https://doi.org/10.1080/10911359.2016.1273682

Schiele, J. H. (1996). Afrocentricity: An emerging paradigm in social work practice. *Social Work, 41*(3), 284–294. http://www.jstor.org/stable/23718171

CHAPTER 7

TEN COMMANDMENTS FOR ADJUNCTS

Erica Heflin-Queen

ABSTRACT

Adjunct faculty face several challenges. However, once a position is obtained, there are several "rules" one must adhere to increase their longevity as adjuncts. Through the theme of the Notorious B.I.G.'s 2007 hit, "The Ten Crack Commandments," these 10 commandments for adjuncts are based on the experiences of an adjunct with over 13 years of experience at various colleges and universities.

My name is Dr. Erica Heflin-Queen. I have been an educator for 22 years as a classroom teacher, reading specialist, and literacy coach. My interests include educational leadership, teaching reading, and hip-hop pedagogy in the classroom. For as long as I can remember, I have always wanted to teach at the collegiate level. As a young undergraduate student at Morgan State University, a historically Black college in Baltimore, Maryland, I was fortunate to have encountered some of the best professors in all of my courses, from the general education requirements to those in the teacher

Don't Forget About the Adjuncts!, pages 73–79
Copyright © 2023 by Information Age Publishing
www.infoagepub.com
All rights of reproduction in any form reserved.

education department where I was an elementary education major. I was inspired by their knowledge, ability to connect with students, and how they pushed and prepared us as preservice teachers to go out into the world and educate students. Teaching is not easy, yet I feel I was more prepared for the challenges that teachers face because of the strong foundation I received at Morgan State. It was during this time that my dream of becoming a classroom teacher grew into wanting to teach at the college level. I wanted to do for others, what Morgan had done for me. What I found through my research was that if I wanted to teach at the college level, I would need to obtain my doctorate degree. So, it was decided. I would finish my studies at Morgan, teach elementary school for a few years to get my master's degree, and finally, get my doctorate degree—all before the age of 35.

What really happened was that I completed my elementary education degree, finished my master's degree 3 years later, and then life happened. I did not enroll right away into a doctoral program, and I did not complete my doctorate until 15 years later. However, I learned that with my master's degree in reading, I could teach at the community college level. This opened doors for me tremendously, as I found that my experience as a classroom teacher, coupled with my experience and specialization in reading, would allow me to teach not only a plethora of teacher education courses geared towards preparing new teachers, but also, it would afford me the opportunity to teach developmental reading and writing courses, which is one of the most important courses that students will register for at every school of higher education in the country.

My biggest challenge as an adjunct has been in attempting to secure a position. After submitting my resume to several community colleges in 2005, I waited for years to be called. Every year, I would update my resume, email someone in the department, and wait. Nothing happened. It was not all the submissions that got me the job. Ultimately, it was a personal connection that helped me obtain my first adjunct opportunity.

It was during my graduate courses for my post-master's degree that I met a very nice woman whom I bonded with very quickly. It turned out that she was the director of teacher education at one of the schools that I had applied to. One day while having a conversation, I told her that I was looking into adjunct opportunities, and she passed my name and resume along to one of her coordinators who unexpectedly called me one day to offer me a position teaching a reading course. I jumped at the opportunity, and a wonderful professional relationship began. From then on, she would email me each semester and ask me if I was willing to teach that same course. It was then that I learned the first rule of being an adjunct, a prerequisite if you will—networking is key. It helps if you know someone. I tried for years to get my foot in the door, and even with all of my qualifications, it still took for someone who knew someone to pass my name along for me to actually be offered a position. This connection that I made helped jumpstart my career as an adjunct professor.

I kept my day job as a reading specialist and I taught face-to-face classes in the evenings several days each week. As a single mother, that was very challenging, but I had a support system that helped me in the evenings. Thankfully, times have changed and there are many more opportunities to teach remotely—no babysitter required. I currently teach many courses within the teacher education department at several colleges, as well as developmental reading courses within the English department. As an adjunct with over 10 years of experience, I have learned a lot along the way. In the spirit of the Notorious B.I.G's "Ten Crack Commandments" (2017) and through the lens of hip hop pedagogy (Rose, 2018), I will share with you what I feel are the 10 commandments for adjuncts, based on my experience.

TEN COMMANDENTS FOR ADJUNCTS

Rule 1—Never Let No One Know How Much Dough You Hold

Securing adjunct positions can be pretty difficult, and bragging about how many courses you have secured may not go over well with fellow adjuncts who are scrambling for coursework. Therefore, do not brag to other adjuncts about the courses that you are teaching. Furthermore, you can have one semester where you are in high demand and teaching multiple courses, and the following semester you may find yourself with one or zero courses to teach. It all depends on enrollment. Stay humble.

Rule 2—Never Let Them Know Your Next Move

This rule pairs well with Rule 1. Have some discretion as to how many courses you are teaching to colleagues who are not close to you. Again, jobs are difficult to find and keep, so the less competition that you have, the better. If your colleagues aren't in the same field, then, share away, if you must. But if they are, you may not want to always disclose where the next adjunct opportunity is coming from. Because they may try to steal your opportunity!

Rule 3—Never Trust Nobody

This rule pertains to documenting all of your communication with students and faculty. As a professional, you must always keep the lines of communication open with students. Make sure that you have documentation in your course syllabus as to when you will reply to a student's email. If you communicate with a student via phone, follow up to the phone call with an email that summarizes the call. Always have documentation to support how much you have communicated with students and faculty. Basically, make sure you have receipts.

Rule 4—Never Get High On Your Own Supply

Once you have secured a position as an adjunct, it is okay to celebrate! It may have taken you several years to get the call! However, stay focused because the position can be taken away from you in a heartbeat. A college may need you one semester, and not the next. Enjoy the position while you have it, however, you need to always think about how you are going to set yourself apart from the other adjuncts in the department to increase your chances of being welcomed to return the following semester. It is always important to remain humble in anything that you do, and as adjunct, it is no different.

What I learned was that I needed to be prepared to answer "yes" anytime I was asked to teach a course, and that I needed to figure out childcare later. If you are asked to teach a course, and you are unable to take the position, the dean will simply hang up the phone with you and call the next person on their list, who will surely say yes. And once someone else takes the course and teaches it, they will forever be asked to teach the course, while your name will surely be forgotten. Don't allow that to happen. As much as possible, be prepared to say "yes" when offered a course for the following semester. If you want to keep adjuncting at that particular school, you must be available as soon as the phone call is received or the email pops up in your inbox.

Rule 5—Never Sell Crack Where You Rest At

While this rule applies to Biggie's alternative ventures, as an adjunct, I interpret this as, as an adjunct, you to need to branch out and apply for opportunities in places that you may not have normally sought out opportunities. Sure, the neighborhood community college is great, and if there are positions open there you should by all means, apply. However, you should also look for opportunities that may be a bit further down the road. I have applied to every community college within a 50-mile radius, which at times meant that I was driving an hour to adjunct. There are so many more asynchronous and synchronous remote opportunities to adjunct more than ever, so it should be even easier to find adjunct opportunities that are further out from where you live. There may also be unique opportunities with online colleges and programs. Explore them all.

Rule 6—Credit? Dead It

If you think that teaching as an adjunct is going to make you rich, you should consider a new occupation. You will not make a lot of money as an adjunct. You will not receive medical benefits. One must strictly teach for the love of the position. Just recently, UCLA made headlines for their advertisement for an adjunct who would be paid a zero-dollar salary (Hartocollis, 2022). Many adjuncts teach at several colleges to make ends meet. If one is expecting to get rich or quit their day job, they should be prepared. An adjunct position will not get you there.

Rule 7—Keep Your Family and Business Completely Separated

As an adjunct professor, you will teach many students from all walks of life. In most cases, mixing family and teaching is fine. However, watch out for family or friends that need to secure a few credits to keep their certification and who may want to enroll in your class to what they feel may be an "easy A." In this situation, it may be best to suggest to your family or friend that they enroll in a separate course section, to eliminate this occurrence, and to salvage the relationship that you have with that family member or friend.

Rule 8—Never Keep No Weight on You

The weight Biggie was speaking of is entirely different than the weight of an adjunct. However, I interpret this as how adjuncts (especially those working full-time jobs), can find themselves weighed down by the demands of working full time and working as an adjunct on the side. Therefore, self-care is the key to survival. The load of an adjunct can be heavy. Grading discussion boards, assignments, projects, and exams, is a lot of work if you are truly giving students meaningful feedback for their work. It is of the utmost importance that an adjunct takes the time to rest, relax, and focus on themselves.

Rule 9—If You Ain't Getting a Badge Stay Away From Police

Stay professionally developed, surround yourself with people who contribute to your work, and do not distract it, and opportunities may find their way to you. You never know where the next opportunity to teach a course will come from. I once was able to secure an adjunct position just from conversing with someone on Twitter. I had no idea this person was in charge of hiring, however, it was through our social media communication that I learned that he was in need of someone to teach a course in his department which I just happened to have certification. With that said, be mindful of your social media footprint and what you say online. It can not only help you get a job, but also, it can lead to one being taken away.

Rule 10—Consignment

This final rule in Biggie's song warns against consignment. In the adjunct world, I interpret that as giving away your knowledge and your presentations that you have created for free. Trading and sharing the courses you have created can be very helpful, just make sure you are receiving the same in return. Remember your worth and your abilities. At times, one may feel like they do not have as much worth as a full-time faculty member and that the content and courses they have created do not matter. This is simply untrue. Know your worth, demand payment and recognition for your contributions to the courses that you teach. You matter.

CONCLUSION

Adjunct faculty face a set of unique challenges, such as lack of equitable pay, benefits, and course load (Buch et al., 2017; Charlier & Williams, 2011; Lerner, 2014; Washington, 2012). Nevertheless, being an adjunct can be very rewarding as well. As an adjunct you are able to share the knowledge base that you have with students and prepare them for their future careers. However, one must know that landing the first adjunct opportunity can be challenging. It may take time, and patience is key. Once an adjunct position is secured, work hard, stay focused, and try to never turn down an opportunity when asked to teach a course. I keep these commandments close, and I find it easier to remember them by reciting them in my head through the voice and melody of the Notorious B.I.G's song. Follow the 10 commandments, and you will surely be successful.

REFERENCES

Buch, K. K., McCullough, H., & Tamberelli, L. (2017). Understanding and responding to the unique needs and challenges facing adjunct faculty: A longitudinal study. *International Journal of Learning, Teaching and Educational Research, 16*(10), 27–40. https://doi.org/10.26803/ijlter

Charlier, H. D., & Williams, M. R. (2011). The reliance on and demand for adjunct faculty members in America's rural, suburban, and urban community colleges. *Community College Review, 39*(2), 160–180. https://doi.org/10.1177/0091552111405839

Hartocollis, A. (2022, April 6). Help wanted: Adjunct professor, must have doctorate. Salary: $0. *New York Times.* https://www.nytimes.com/2022/04/06/us/ucla-adjunct-professor-salary.html

Lerner, M. (2014, April 15). Adjunct professors learn hard truth about faculty jobs. *Buffalo News.*

Rose, C. (2018). Toward a critical hip-hop pedagogy for teacher education. In C. Emdin & E. Adjapong (Eds.), *#HipHopEd: The compilation on hip-hop education* (pp. 27–37). Brill. https://doi.org/10.1163/9789004371873_004

The Notorious B. I. G. (1997). Ten crack commandments [Song]. On *Life After Death.* DJ Premier.

Washington, A. T. (2012, December 20). The adjunct carousel. *Diverse issues in higher education, 29*(23), 34–36. https://www.proquest.com/docview/1265769585?accountid=11292&forcedol=true

CHAPTER 8

WHAT ADJUNCT FACULTY NEED TO BE SUCCESSFUL IN THE *ONLINE* CLASSROOM?

Lealan M. Zaccone
Sandra C. Hannigan

ABSTRACT

In this chapter we discuss what it takes to be a successful *online* adjunct and focus on the importance of online instruction, communication, support, and teaching in the *online* classroom. We are two very enthusiastic and committed online instructors who collectively have over 30 years' experience in higher education administration, instructional technology, student affairs, and online teaching. We believe that online instruction is a powerful teaching methodology that when facilitated well can be used as a successful teaching platform similar to the traditional classroom approach. As adjunct faculty we aspire to teach every online class with tools, technology, and techniques designed for success. In this chapter we explore the challenges and opportunities specific to the online learning environment. Topics include laying the groundwork for online teaching (i.e., onboarding, trainings, expectations, & other administrative "stuff"), how to manage your course and time, and establish a network of support (i.e., know your platform, learners, technolo-

Don't Forget About the Adjuncts!, pages 81–94
Copyright © 2023 by Information Age Publishing
www.infoagepub.com
All rights of reproduction in any form reserved.

81

gies, & community). In conclusion, we share tips and tricks for online teaching (with resources!) and provide encouragement on how to be a successful online adjunct.

Over the years online teaching and learning has gained momentum. Today, people in general are experiencing flexible work schedules, increased gas prices and rent, and a need for affordable education. In addition, lifestyles have changed, schedules are remote, and learning is everywhere. As a result, many faculty are joining the ranks to teach online. With growing opportunities for teaching online, there is also a demand to prepare adjunct faculty on how to teach successfully in the online learning environment. Thus, it is important to address the unique motivations, needs, and teaching techniques specific to the online classroom.

WHO ARE "WE?"

My name is Lealan Zaccone and I am an adjunct online professor at Northampton Community College in Bethlehem, Pennsylvania and head psychology instructor for international students at Washington and Thornton Academy. I've worked in higher education administration for over 20 years, specializing in the community college environment, and provided teaching and learning opportunities for training and support for online education. As a higher education professional my passion is to foster quality experiences that promote a rich community of learners. In my previous positions as associate director of online learning, I provided faculty training and support for teaching with technology, understanding online pedagogy and quality practices for online teaching and learning. Additionally, I co-facilitated and designed an online teaching orientation to assist all new online adjunct to teach online and provided them with the allocation of resources needed to succeed throughout their first teaching semester. I am strongly committed to providing the support and services needed for quality online teaching and helping students achieve academic success. My goal is to continue to collaborate with faculty and students to deliver and support quality educational experiences.

I am Sandra Hannigan (Sandy), an instructional technologist and adjunct faculty instructor at Northampton Community College (NCC) in Bethlehem, PA. I began my employment at NCC in 2009. I had recently moved to the Lehigh Valley after living in the Kansas City area due to my husband's transfer. I am originally from New Jersey where I began my professional teaching experience which I continued in the Midwest. While there, I earned a master's degree in teaching with a focus on technology in the classroom, taught junior high school students, and moved on to teach in a corporate environment as a global training manager and instructional designer. It was at this time that I also became an adjunct instructor at two community colleges. In 2012 at NCC, my tech department merged with the online learning department. In addition to my instructional technologist duties, I served as an adjunct teaching an introduction to information technology course in two different modalities. I still enjoy teaching this course today! It was during this time that Lealan and I joined forces to improve the onboarding training for potential adjuncts at NCC.

The "we" that is referenced in this writing is Lealan Zaccone and Sandy Hannigan.

OPPORTUNITIES AND CHALLENGES

Both faculty and students appreciate the convenience of online instruction. Some *even* prefer connecting with technology. Remote learning, just in time delivery, and "anytime, anyplace" instruction requires an abundance of self-management and motivation for both students and faculty. Benefits include online collaboration, flexible formats, and quick access to a rich pool of resources. However, with the title of virtual learning, there is also a strong need for discipline, dedication, and imagination to keep students engaged. It takes willingness to develop relationships through technology and a strong commitment to navigate various technologies and platforms. As an online adjunct, you must strike a balance when establishing and maintaining predictable patterns that prevent an expectation of 24/7 access and burnout.

EFFECTIVE ONLINE TEACHING STRATEGIES

Creating and Adhering to a Syllabus

Your syllabus is an academic contract to ensure that your objectives and criteria for assessing work are clear and detailed enough for learners to understand what is expected of them. Include a statement of academic honesty and integrity expectations and consequences for dishonesty early in your online course. I (Zaccone) involve my learners in defining and committing to an honors code of honesty and integrity by signing their name to an official document. It is also important for courses to provide information on academic policies, conduct, guidelines, cheating policies, grading, and assessments.

Managing Day-to-Day Struggles

Be explicit and detailed in the syllabus about course management and participation guidelines. Make sure expectations are clear to all learners at the onset of the course. Reinforce due dates, schedules, and timelines. Post materials and conduct activities on a preset schedule. Allow learners to keep track of their own progress. By staying organized, you model the behavior you would like to see from your learners. Create clear and concise grading rubrics that define what is expected in each assignment as well as how the final grade will be calculated. Model the expected behavior in discussion postings and in sample responses.

Pacing the Class Appropriately

Be noticeably present in the course. Pace the class appropriately by assessing learning frequently, grading often, and providing early feedback so learners have time to adjust behaviors. This is a good practice for any online course since it helps the learners' pace themselves in the asynchronous environment. Some techniques include posting answers to frequently asked questions or generic feedback for assignments. Also use the class comments section or the generic feedback section in the quizzes tool to address questions that come up repeatedly. Additionally, you can keep and reuse news items and announcements along with other communication (recording, images, comments) from one offering of the course to the next. Many online instructors have also adapted classroom assessment for their online courses to assess learning frequently by using classroom assessment techniques (CATs; https://cft.vanderbilt.edu/guides-sub-pages/cats/)

Opening and Closing Each Class Effectively

Send an introductory welcome letter to each student prior to or at the start of the semester. The letter should explain a little bit about yourself and how to access the class and begin work. In addition, make personal contact with each student through email or synchronous chat to communicate throughout the semester. Encourage students to communicate with you and provide regular, personalized announcements and communication throughout the course (start and end of semester, even beyond). Some of my (Zaccone) favorite feedback comes from alumni who contact me after graduation and in their current career.

> **Faculty Tip:**
> Be willing to commit your time, energy, and passion for teaching to your online course; make tweaks and adjustments before, during, and after every course. I tell my students every semester that we are in this environment learning together. Online faculty must be willing to give control up to the class and to the students—always, of course, with the direction and guidance of the faculty.
>
> —Lealan Zaccone, Online Adjunct,
Introduction to Psychology and Student Success (2022)

Testing and Grading Strategies

Use multiple assessment methods, not only tests and quizzes but also interactive discussions, written assignments, case studies, projects, reports, presentations, role plays, and self-check quizzes. A greater reliance on written and other more subjective assessments is recommended for online teaching as personalized, authentic assessments make cheating less feasible. For example, annotated bibliographies with annotations that explain how the sources inspired a learner's research is a good strategy to ensure both quality resources and individualized discovery. In addition, some online instructors provide learners with rubrics and/or examples of quality work as well as resources for good citation examples (Stavredes, 2011).

Finding a Faculty Mentor and Leaning on Peers as You Prepare and Teach Your First Online Semester

Other adjunct faculty are the best resource to draw upon for advice on any questions you may have about online teaching. Moreover, it is equally important to share your experiences, learning, or content with others to create a community of online scholars.

> Collaboration among colleagues is important, and I have learned so much about teaching and learning when I have shared my own experiences with others and heard about their experiences, too. I've learned new activities and have heard great advice about class management issues. If anything, it's rewarding to be able to talk to others who understand what I'm going through. (Everson, 2009, para. 54)

Improving and Learning From Student Evaluations

Gather feedback from your students about what works and what does not work. Ask them how the online course and resources can improve.

Take their enthusiasm, experience, and knowledge and adapt to it. The best teachers are lifelong learners themselves, constantly evolving, so any information that leads to improvement should be valued and listened to. What keeps me (Hannigan) motivated teaching online is the feedback I get from my students and most importantly from my Dean. From the formal evaluations, course observation and positive feedback I receive I am always motivated to do better.

Debunking Common Online Teaching Myths

There are still many opinions regarding the quality of online teaching. But,

> with any teaching assignment, if you believe in the purpose, if you see value in what it is you do, you will naturally be better at it. That's why I suggest teachers who are uncertain about the value of online education take an online class for themselves. Not necessarily to "get on board" but to at least develop a clearer understanding of what the thing they fear, or dislike actually *is*. Often, the traditional instructors who have a negative view of online teaching express that they had a better online learning experience than they had anticipated. (Shriner, 2015b, para. 6)

LAYING THE GROUNDWORK FOR ONLINE TEACHING

Online adjuncts bring an array of talent, experience, and expertise to the online classroom. They also serve as recruitment advocates for prospective students (anywhere, everywhere) and help connect knowledge to an online classroom from anywhere in the world. The skills needed to teach online are a comfort level with technology, independent curriculum development, dependable communication, and a willingness to commit time and interactivity with students. In addition, it is important for an online adjunct to have academic goals clearly stated prior to the start of a semester.

Adjuncts must be able to know where to find resources and receive adequate training and access to ongoing support throughout the semester. They are required to know the institution, the administrative processes, pedagogical expectations, developmental opportunities, and student demographic profile. Orienting adjuncts helps develop communication within their institution, identify gaps in their knowledge and preparation, and empowerment to excel in the online classroom. Topics include curriculum organization, knowledge of the learning management system (LMS), awareness of contractual duties and responsibilities, securing course material and proprietary websites, incorporation of student evaluation and division feedback, important registration dates, course administration, outreach and retention, student complaint process, grade appeals, and point of contact (i.e., Get to know your dean!; Shriner, 2015a).

Online faculty must learn how to be an online learner themselves. According to several online faculty in the field of online teaching, "Those who teach most successfully online are those who understand what it was like to be an online student with an enthusiasm for learning how to teach from that process" (Collision et al., 2000, p. 34). When Sandy and I first began teaching online as online adjuncts at the local community college, we were presented with a high-quality onboarding experience that helped streamline all administrative processes. We also developed and received a thorough and applicable online teaching orientation on how to use the essential tools and features of a course management system.

An orientation program performs multiple functions. Good training programs

> familiarize teachers with the unique needs of the adult online learner, offer guidance when it comes to facilitating effective and engaging discussion boards, share ideas about bringing material to life through interactivity, and go over the benefits and problems associated with using outside technologies in the classroom. (Farnsworth & Bevis, 2006, p. 25)

They serve as an introduction to staff, services, and support, and provide an overview of curriculum, policy updates, and implementation practices. They also help to establish a faculty support group, develop a network, maintain relationships with colleagues, and exchange ideas.

Supporting online adjuncts at a distance is essential to the success of online teaching. Because many are geographically remote, online faculty do not always have access to a network or mentor in proximity to them. They do not have somebody just down the hall that they can go to with their teaching questions. They are basically isolated, working in a remote environment. Oftentimes, they are teaching multiple online classes for different institutions, adapting to different online platforms and interactive technology tools that are constantly changing. When you start to combine all these factors—working alone, minimal support, high-paced environment in something totally new—it becomes very challenging for an adjunct faculty to really feel prepared and supported.

Online orientations help online faculty

> become more comfortable with common learning management systems (like Blackboard, Canvas, or Moodle). You learn how to use them effectively and with all the bells and whistles that could bring your learning objectives to life. Good training programs will familiarize teachers with the unique needs of the adult online learner, offer guidance when it comes to facilitating effective

and engaging discussion boards, share ideas about bringing material to life through interactivity, video/voice-over, and so on, and go over the benefits and problems associated with using outside technologies in the classroom. (Shriner, 2015b, para. 14).

In addition, saving and managing time is especially important in the online teaching environment. Taking extra care of developing an easy-to-follow syllabus is critical for success. The course syllabus

should be peer-reviewed, published, up-to-date, detailed, and comprehensive, with overall and weekly learning outcomes clearly documented. It is important that the syllabus focus not on 'covering a list of topics,' but rather developing competencies and abilities to apply processes within different contexts. (Farnsworth & Bevis, 2006, p. 38)

Carefully review and communicate policies such as technologies used in the online classroom, attendance, online presence, grading scale, timely feedback, online classroom etiquette, and IT support.

MANAGING COURSE AND TIME

Many online courses are asynchronous. Class time is distributed, discussions are ongoing, and feedback is daily. Students work on activities online in their own time at various times (generally week-by-week). Students interact with each other through discussion boards, small group projects, and/or the chat feature with an LMS. Instructor check-in with students individually via assignment feedback tools, office hours, email, and chat is important. Although online faculty are not required to login 24/7, they are required to have a frequent presence. However, many faculty feel obligated to log in multiple times a day, including evenings and weekends, to monitor the online discussions and activities, making it more difficult to distinguish between "class work" and personal time (Wolpert-Gawron, 2017). An effective online instructor develops a pattern for being present throughout the class. The basis for teaching online includes a strong emphasis on content, pedagogy, and assessment with careful planning on all three.

Here are some time management strategies to build into good online teaching practices.

- Write clearly and concisely so learners understand expectations and directions. Also, organize content in an easy-to-follow order.
- Be explicit about time requirements in the syllabus, such as assignment due dates, discussion participation timelines, virtual office hours, and response times to e-mails.

What Adjunct Faculty Need to Be Successful in the Online Classroom? ▪ 89

- Allocate set amounts of time for working on the course. Resist the temptation to be available "24/7." Adjust a schedule to monitor the course around assignments and exams.
- Establish a "day off" during the week. For example, announce to the learners you will not be checking the course activities at all on Saturdays.
- Set virtual office hours and keep them to chat or conference questions.
- Set a maximum turnaround time for grading and feedback so learners know when to expect. Students tend to be more patient waiting for a response when patterns are set.
- Log into your course at least once a day during the regular work week. A regular schedule of brief logins keeps up with messages and saves time in the long run (Shelton & Saltsman, 2004).

Overall, effective online adjuncts:

Know where to go for help. Online adjuncts should be familiar with who are the points of contacts at the leading institution and who to go to for assistance for their online classroom to run smoothly on all levels (i.e., know your instructional designer, help desk assistant, division contact, department head, student affairs leaders, library and resource assistants, and financial and payroll personnel).

Focus on pedagogy, rather than medium (video, simulation, text, etc.) to stimulate effective instruction. For example, three questions to consider when creating engaging asynchronous materials. How do I provoke, discover, and generalize learning?

Present detailed written instructions and concise learning objectives in your course. Write clearly so learners understand expectations and directions. Also, organize content and documents in an easy to follow

---

Faculty Tip:
An effective online adjunct provides clear instructions, prompt responses, constructive feedback, empathy and kindness, diversity in assignments, a clear and detailed syllabus, weekly announcement, reminders, and communication. After the start of every semester, I always review student evaluations and make changes accordingly. In addition, I create an electronic "Feel Good Folder" highlighting student comments. When times get challenging in online teaching, I reflect on these comments and use them as motivation to keep pressing on!

—Lealan Zaccone, Online Adjunct
Introduction to Psychology, Student Success (2022)

order. Clear writing and organization help to avoid confusion and can save hours of clarification later.

Be a regular and dependable online correspondent. Set the tone and demeanor with your communication to model for learners an appropriate communication style. Define what is acceptable language and tone and what will not be tolerated. Establish the rules of netiquette for your course.

Facilitate effective interaction and collaborative activities using institution's platforms. There are many amazing tools that can be used in an online course, but it is important to be vigilant about identifying what is necessary to achieve your learning goals.

> Instructors need to know their content, become a student of their own content, take their own tests and assignments. Video, audio, and animation all have their place but if the tools don't work, they can cause barriers and negativity on course materials. If you are using 3rd party materials, be sure content and due dates are current and don't reflect last semester's dates. Get to know your customer representative so that you can go to them for assistance. If you need to change your syllabus or content, advise your class. (Hannigan)

Be willing and able to commit time daily to the online class. Students appreciate regular communication and timely feedback on their progress. It is important to establish a "teacher presence" letting students know that you are available to them. Set your parameters for doing so. I (Hannigan) advise my students that if they send me an email at 10:30 p.m. or later, I won't answer it until the next morning. Let them know how you can be reached as well, by phone, text or email.

Humanize connection and create community right from the start. Choose a "warm" tone and use positive and friendly language. It helps to share personal experiences and always show enthusiasm for the course and content. I (Zaccone) strive to create a supportive online community where students can be free to take risks in discussion, attempting to explain an understanding of concepts and ideas from the start of the class. I offer an icebreaker activity to get students accustomed to collaboration. I then relate their early contributions to future topics we cover in class.

Seek out ongoing training opportunities to stay up to date with the latest trends and technology, not only in your field of study but also in the field of online education. Share ideas, collaborate, and commiserate about the online teaching experience.

Don't hesitate to reach out to others who teach online to share ideas, collaborate, and commiserate about your experiences (Ko & Rossen, 2004).

ONLINE TEACHING TAKEAWAYS

Your institution may offer professional development or have faculty support groups, adjunct faculty centers or teaching and learning think tanks that online adjuncts can take advantage of. Many colleges and universities offer workshops on teaching pedagogies as well as how to incorporate technology into the classroom. Additionally, local school districts and community centers also serve as a useful resource. Here are a few resources for best practices in faculty development for online teaching:

- Northampton Community College Start of the Semester Resource for Online Faculty (https://docs.google.com/presentation/d/16q9WonqZT-esivlqYgBhXaxNgoRoBY0hMc6JI9K-TSas/edit).
- Bucks County Community College Online Learning Tips (BOLT) (https://bucks.instructure.com/courses/32946/pages/a-canvas-resource-site-for-bucks-instructors).
- St. Mary's College of California Faculty Development (https://www.stmarys-ca.edu/faculty-development/resources-for-faculty).
- Nationwide Remote Teaching Resources (Comprehensive Google Doc): (https://docs.google.com/spreadsheets/d/1VT9oiNYPyiEsGHBoDKlwLlWAsWP58sGV7A3oIuEUG3k/htmlview?usp=sharing&cid=nwsltrtn&source=ams&sourceId=4700735)

Faculty Tip:
Keep your students engaged by adding technology in your course. Provide students with choices when submitting assignments; Record your own announcements for the week instead of sending through email; Take a virtual class trip; Reach out to others that are teaching the same course for fresh ideas; Remember: Always have a Plan B—technology isn't perfect! Give it a try.
—Sandy Hannigan, Online Adjunct
Instructional Technologist. Intro to Information Technology (2022)

The LMS is an integral platform for teaching online and there are many to choose from. An LMS enables faculty to develop quality courses and instruction while maintaining consistency throughout the institution. Undoubtedly your institution has already chosen which LMS will be available to you. Therefore, you need to be up-to-speed on its usage to leverage all the advantages and opportunities that the LMS can deliver. You should begin by exploring the positive additions an LMS can provide for your class and then seeking out those who can assist you with using it.

> **Faculty Tip:**
> Remember the purpose for using technology in your course. It should be used to enhance the concept, engage students, and appeal to different learning styles. Incorporate *Gaming* tools such as *Kahoot* to use as a chapter review. Instead of a written discussion board, try creating a *Padlet* so students can visually review responses. By using alternate techniques students will remain engaged and encourage collaboration.
> — Sandy Hannigan, Online Adjunct
> Instructional Technologist. Intro to Information Technology (2022)

Organizing content carefully and consistently. Your LMS will have a "Help" section for you to review on how to incorporate tools (i.e., discussion boards, tests, and surveys)

Providing your students with unlimited access to required learning materials. Assure that assignments are available 24/7 and if they are time-sensitive, assure that students are aware of their availability. For example, if a reading assignment is only available for a particular week, check that the availability dates are set correctly so that the students have access to them. We all know that students work during many different hours of the day.

Assessing and tracking learner performance and progress. It is the instructor's duty to keep track of students' grades. You should develop your own system for tracking and stick to it. If your LMS, for example, has a tool for alerting you to *at-risk* students, utilize it. The earlier in the semester you do this, the sooner the student can get back on track. Feedback and communication here is very important. Make it a habit to check the grade center daily and most importantly check it soon after an assignment or test is due. Also, impart upon your students that it is their responsibility to track their own grades.

Integrating social learning experiences. Encourage relationship-building learning by asking learners to share information about themselves, such as hobbies and favorite music, incorporate it into lessons. Share something about yourself in return.

Conferences are another way to obtain knowledge in the field of online teaching. Take advantage of virtual webinars and conferences (many are free) from book publishers such as Cengage and McGraw Hill. Sign up for newsletters from technology companies whose products you are interested in. Look for institutions in your immediate area that offer webinars and symposiums. Some nationally recognized conferences and seminars include the International Society for Technology in Education which helps educators around the world use technology for solutions in teaching online (https://www.iste.org/). Educause is a nonprofit association and the largest community of technology, academic, industry, and campus leaders advancing higher education using IT (https://www.educause.edu/). The Future of Education Technology Conference gathers the most dynamic and innovative education leaders and professionals from around the world for an intensive, highly collaborative exploration of modern technologies, best practices, and pressing issues in education and teaching (https://www.fetc.org/). MERLOT system provides access to curated online learning and support materials and content creation tools, led by an international community of educators, learners, and researchers. (https://www.merlot.org/merlot/). Annually, the online teaching conference is a premier gathering of faculty, staff, and administrators who are leading the way in developing innovative and effective online education. As an inter-segmental conference focused on curriculum, pedagogy, and technology to improve online instruction, learning, and student success (http://onlineteachingconference.org/).

Most colleges allow you to teach online with a graduate degree in your field of study. After years of study, you are considered a subject matter expert, fully prepared to impart your information through lecture. However, it is always an innovative idea to pursue an online teaching certificate that will help you design your online course and improve your face-to-face courses as well. When you have a stronger knowledge of teaching pedagogy, you will be able to see the correlation between learning objectives, learning activities, and assessments. This will prepare you for converting your curriculum to an online format. Several colleges and universities even offer 4- or 5-week online teaching certificate courses. Taking a course such as this would be considered professional development. Additional online teaching qualifications include: Online Teaching Certification Trainings (https://online learningconsortium.org/learn/teaching-certificates/); Fundamentals of Online Teaching (https://pdc.wisc.edu/noncredit/fundamentals-of-online -teaching/); Quality Matters Training (https://www.qualitymatters.org/); and Adjunct Worlds Online Teaching Certificate (https://adjunctworld .com/blog/adjunctworlds-online-teacher-training-ot-101/).

In conclusion, we would add that online teaching and teaching in general is a long-term and ever-evolving learning experience for you that will impact your students. The more enthusiasm you provide about the subject matter content and your willingness to embrace innovative technologies and modalities will improve student engagement, collaboration, and the overall success of your online class. Reading this chapter is proof enough that you are willing to move forward on your journey to online teaching and learning. We wish you the best of luck!

REFERENCES

Collison, G., Elbaum, B., Haavind, S., & Tinker, R. (2000). *Facilitating online learning: Effective strategies for moderators.* Atwood Publishing.

Everson, M. (2009, September). *10 things I've learned about teaching online.* https://elearnmag.acm.org/featured.cfm?aid=1609990

Farnsworth, K., & Bevis, T. B. (2006). *A fieldbook for community college online instructors.* Community College Press. https://eric.ed.gov/?id=ED499836

Ko, S., & Rossen, S. (2004). *Teaching online: A practical guide* (2nd ed.). Houghton Mifflin.

Shelton, K., & Saltsman, G. (2004). Tips and tricks for teaching online: How to teach like a pro. *Instructional Technology and Distance Learning, 1*(10). https://www.itdl.org/Journal/Oct_04/article04.htm

Shriner, B. (2015a, May 22). *5 things effective online instructors know.* https://adjunctworld.com/blog/5-things-effective-online-instructors-know/

Shriner, B. (2015b, May 6). *7 characteristics of effective online teachers.* https://adjunctworld.com/blog/7-characteristics-of-effective-online-teachers/

Stavredes, T. (2011). *Effective online teaching: Foundations and strategies for student success.* Wiley & Sons.

Wolpert-Gawron, H. (2017, September 27). *Extending classroom management online: Nine suggestions to help you provide online learners with class norms and expectations and a sense of community.* https://www.edutopia.org/article/extending-classroom-management-online

CHAPTER 9

THE INVISIBLE EDUCATOR

Are Adjunct Teachers Undervalued?

Raleta S. Dawkins
Sabrina Hinton
Saleena Frazier

ABSTRACT

In many cases, adjunct professors hold graduate and doctoral degrees while teaching at the collegiate level. Often our experiences allow us to consider the stresses and benefits of working higher education. Adjunct professors bring experience from various backgrounds. Some come from the corporate sector; some are entrepreneurs, administrators, or retired faculty. As adjunct professors, we are a driving force that keeps many departments afloat and running. However, we often serve as temporary employees who work on a part-time contract basis. While adjuncts do not have the same responsibilities as full-time, tenured professors, they implement many of the "regular" tasks associated with teaching university courses. We know our roles as adjunct professors are essential to successful student learning in traditional and online courses just as much as full-time faculty. However, adjunct professors often receive less respect than their full-time faculty counterparts. Nevertheless, our roles are considered oversimplified. At some point, adjunct professors realize

Don't Forget About the Adjuncts!, pages 95–103
Copyright © 2023 by Information Age Publishing
www.infoagepub.com
All rights of reproduction in any form reserved.

that we have suffered an injustice, and there is a lack of comprehensive data regarding our importance.

INTRODUCTION TO THE AUTHORS

Although we are adjunct professors, we dually work other careers throughout the mid-Atlantic region of the United States. We, the authors, have invested more than 10 years of servicing across teaching, and supporting students and departments across multiple learning environments. We teach at historically Black colleges and universities, primarily White institutions, technical colleges, and private and for-profit colleges. As adjuncts, we cultivated practical instructional experiences for students by providing high-quality face-to-face instruction for preservice teachers and students seeking opportunities to serve as early care professionals. In recent times, it has been necessary to thoughtfully embrace the COVID-19 pandemic to expand our teaching capacities taking advantage of teaching remotely for educational institutions outside our physical location. Like full-time faculty, we have endured the struggles and joys of migrating to the new normal of developing online, hybrid, and synchronous learning environments. We often redeveloped such courses without pay or an ounce of gratitude from the full-time faculty we support.

As new "PhDers," we were excited and eager to take on adjunct work. Over the years, we have worked to perfect the art of adjuncting by teaching and redesigning many courses to meet the changing needs of diverse students. We frequently serve on department committees to show our willingness to serve our departments and gain university experience. As adjunct professors, we hold firm to our commitments to support accreditation processes. We often mentor and coach students while earning low salaries that vary semester to semester with no guarantee of consistent work. In the beginning, the rewards and prestige of being connected to a university teaching position gave us a feeling of success. That is until the time came for them to apply and hope our adjunct experiences would prepare and open opportunities for us to earn a full-time, tenured position. Over the years, we have seen departments across universities run by a sizable adjunct population. However, we have seen a limited number of our adjunct peers selected for faculty positions. The lack of adjunct promotions to full-time faculty positions has caused each of us a painful feeling of being devalued and not respected for our years of service and commitment to the growth of programs. Currently, we feel we are approaching an intersection of deciding if our desire to impact future learners is greater and more rewarding than the lack of respect we have endured.

ADVERSITY AS ADJUNCTS

As adjunct professors, we find teaching on a collegiate level meaningful. We play a significant role in the success of student learning. As we bring much subject matter expertise, professional know-how, and workplace experience to the fields in which we teach. Yet, we can compare ourselves to scarred veterans or underpaid employees with ease. To us, it seems the overall objective of universities is to keep adjunct professors as part-time staff, with no room for growth, no benefits, and no chances to increase our pay. We sometimes feel that administrators and full-time faculty regard us lowly. We feel like unappreciated, second-rate employees even though our educational contributions are necessary. Most adjunct professors offer the same quality learning experiences as full-time faculty, but we often deal with: (a) remaining silent about the injustices we feel have occurred within our departments, (b) having our point of view ignored concerning curriculum and classroom needs, (c) suffering through unpaid vacations, (d) the disappointments of canceled courses, (e) overcoming the chaos of structuring last-minute add-on courses, and (f) the late signing of our contracts to take on regularly scheduled classes.

The first two issues we often face coincide. We feel the innate need to remain silent about the injustices we feel have occurred within our working environments and within each department. Like us, many of our adjunct peers endure problems with student complaints. We often think that if students complain, it will affect our end-of-semester evaluations. For us, this growing concern may hinder us and fellow adjuncts from being asked to return for subsequent semesters.

Similarly, when adjunct professors see issues within departments, our perspectives are not always addressed, taken seriously, or followed up upon. Next, as adjunct professors, we are considered part-time employees. For many of us, this means we do not work enough hours at one university to receive benefits. Although this can be a burden, it does offer us the positive benefit of knowing that we can take a vacation with pay at our leisure. The fourth and fifth issues complement one another. Throughout our tenure as adjunct professors, we have noticed that our departments expect us to be flexible and at their disposal of their departments for the assignment of courses. On one side of the token, we are continuously asked at the last minute to take on additional courses; we often fear that future opportunities will be limited if we do not graciously accept these offers. On the flip side, when courses are taken away from us at the last minute due to a lack of student enrollment, we are expected to be flexible and understand the changes that negatively impact our pay. Such types of course load changes have been frustrating for us. We have experienced that such changes arise when a full-faculty goes on leave or there is a vacant position where they will not promote us.

As adjunct professors, we see ourselves and others slowly losing passion for teaching due to the constraints of the profession. Typically, adjunct professors receive contracts written for one semester at a time. Therefore, we are rarely entitled to receive benefits. To us, this means we do not have an opportunity to secure health insurance, retirement benefits, or any standard employee benefits through the university. These benefits are often obtained through other avenues or by our spouses.

Lack of pay often leads to problems with adjunct retention and job dissatisfaction. The average intermediary salary of adjunct professors is $3,100 per course (American Federation of Teachers [AFT], 2020; Yakoboski, 2016).

We can corroborate this finding as we earn between $20,000 to $25,000 annually, depending on our course loads. Many assume high course loads across more than one university each semester to achieve these salaries. We, like most adjuncts, are part-time in our contracts but usually work full-time schedules to effectively plan, teach, hold office hours, grade, and provide meaningful feedback. When seeing these numbers on paper, it is very disheartening as we personally know some of our full-time counterparts often earn salaries that are double or triple ours for the same number of invested hours per week. For many of our fellow adjuncts, teaching is their only source of household income. We are fortunate as teaching is not. Some data from 2020 showcases that (a) a large portion of adjuncts often live below the federal poverty guideline for a family of four even when our teaching load is higher than our full-time peers; (b) approximately 25% of adjuncts rely on public assistance; (c) another 40% of adjuncts struggle to cover basic household expenses (AFT, 2020; Flaherty, 2020).

When adjunct professors introduce themselves, I often hear a slow, audible "wow." The connotation continually indicates that serving as an adjunct is a bad thing. It can be very irritating when conversations arise, and this terminology is perceived negatively. As adjunct professors, we help our students cultivate the skills necessary to care for and educate their future scholars, who are the future leaders of tomorrow. Helping our students is a skill that should be a part of every educator's DNA, whether adjunct or full-time professors. Reserving the prestige of positively educating college students should be a right of all instructors, adjuncts, and full-time faculty.

In summary, as adjunct professors, we feel little sense of community and are not valued by full-time faculty or the departments we serve. We often feel isolated and disconnected from the goals and mission of our institution and departments. Feelings of isolation are coupled with a disconnection from their full-time faculty peers. These feelings often stem from little things that full-time professors take for granted, such as having personal office space. This one limited resource makes it extremely difficult to hold office hours with students unless it is off-campus or in a common area. We adjunct professors frequently question our job security and lack of development opportunities (Flaherty, 2020). There is no guarantee that adjuncts will be offered a job for the next semester. Lack of job retention tends to make student contact complex and make adjuncts feel less connected and involved compared to their counterparts.

SOME SILVER LINING TO ADJUNCTING

There are many adversities we have faced as adjunct professors. However, we, the authors, are thankful that we have found our "good fit" at our current universities. In this section, we will share several positive experiences that help us decide to continue as adjunct professors. First, we are passionate about our content area. As adjunct professors, we want to contribute to the success of our students. We believe we are knowledgeable assets that bring opportunities for our students to grow in their theoretical understanding and practical, real-world application. Our content area is elementary and early care education. Therefore, many of our students must meet the challenge of creating state and national portfolios prior to graduation. As current classroom educators and administrators, we bring current perspectives of what is going on in modern-day classrooms that can help better equip our students for success in these tasks. Such knowledge sets us apart from full-time faculty. Therefore, many of our students must meet the challenge of creating state and national portfolios prior to graduation. As current classroom educators and administrators, we bring current perspectives of what is going on in modern-day classrooms that can help better equip our students for success in these tasks. Such knowledge sets us apart from full-time faculty. When not stretched too thin by heavy course loads, we frequently find that we can relate to students' needs and effectively provide mentoring and coaching.

Some adjuncts find pleasure in teaching at various locations, universities. For many, we can choose what universities where we work contracts. Having options to work at select universities brings us a sense of freedom. However, we understand that choosing to work at multiple universities is different from having to work at multiple universities to make ends meet. This is one way they see it to increase their pay. Another aspect of freedom is that some adjunct professors desire to teach online courses strictly. In these instances, our need to drive to campus frequently for class and meetings is eliminated by solely teaching online. We, the authors, enjoy having the flexibility and freedom to perform our duties at any time within an asynchronous environment. Another benefit of online teaching is that we can remain mobile without requesting time off.

Finally, as adjunct professors, we have a say in choosing if we want to pursue research and publishing and miss out on the stress of preparing and going through the tenure process. We know full-time professors have a heavy burden with handling their teaching load and functioning on multiple department and university committees. We hear the complaints of our full-time counterparts regarding the tenure process. For tenure, most full-time professors must showcase their strengths in scholarship, service, research, and publications, depending on their university. We enjoy having the freedom to avoid the politics associated with academia. For most adjunct professors, these requirements are not ours. Therefore, we can provide more time for educating students rather than having to attend department and faculty meetings and navigate the bureaucracy.

Whenever an educator introduces themselves as an adjunct, there is always an audible "wow" in the subsequent conversation. This happens because we have been told that it takes a "special individual" to devote their time to teaching. Nevertheless, it has become very irritating with this terminology. As adjuncts, we help our students cultivate the skills necessary to care for and educate our scholars, who are the future leaders of tomorrow. Helping our students is a skill that should be a part of every educator's DNA, but we reserve it for individuals who decide to become adjuncts.

STRATEGIES TO MASTER THE ART OF ADJUNCTING

As adjuncts, we have faced many challenges. However, we have also experienced many successes. From our experiences, we would like to share some tips and strategies we utilize that keep us motivated and dedicated to our positions. As with any career, adjuncts should remain positive and proactive. Teaching requires patience and organization, so it is always best practice to effectively establish working relationships with peers and students. Although complicated at times, collaboration with fellow adjuncts, full-time faculty, and students is vital. Those who work alongside you in academia can potentially serve as resources or partners throughout the semester. Setting the "tone" of the class and coursework expectations for the beginning of the semester can deter student and professor failures. Each of these can eliminate future challenges that are common in classroom environments. In all learning environments, it is best practice to anticipate repetitive challenges that are likely to occur during the course and effectively develop solutions. When these issues are addressed within the course syllabus or during the course introduction, the semester moves a little more smoothly.

We understand the importance of building rapport with students. Since we do not teach every semester, we must gather necessary information concerning our students and assess the continuously changing learning

The Invisible Educator · **101**

environment in which we teach. Taking time to get to know students enables us to orchestrate better-engaging classes that meet various student instructional needs. Finally, adjunct professors should always strive to respond to students concerning coursework, absenteeism, and other issues. We have found that we should always keep clear communication trails and save emails. We must use the features in our learning management systems to send messages, schedule Zoom meetings, and take advantage of all avenues to share information and enable our students to communicate with us, especially when updating students on course requirements. With all the above in mind, we are committed to the work and committed to offering students multiple modes of learning, communication, and submission of assignments.

IMPACTFUL AFFIRMATIONS FOR ADJUNCTS

Positive affirmations are statements spoken out loud, focused on positive wording, and challenging critical thoughts. We can see how using affirmations makes a noticeable change in the sense of presence and self-belief. Thoughts can profoundly impact an adjunct professor's self-esteem and actions. How we speak to ourselves and the words we use in daily life are intrinsically linked to how we feel. As educators, we must nourish ourselves and encourage the same for our students. If we do this, we can rehumanize the learning environments and foster positive relationships within the classrooms that will carry over. As adjunct professors, we must craft guidelines for caring for ourselves and always remember that our health and needs are a priority. We cannot provide exceptional educational experiences if we do not make ourselves a priority within the equation.

We must maintain the mindset that even above course content, we provide guidelines that protect our boundaries to ensure successful sustainability in learning. As adjunct professors, we must nourish ourselves to avoid working in discomfort. We must shape our work environment into one of belonging and vow to dismantle misconceptions of our importance within academia. Here we would like to share some of our favorite affirmations:

- I am making a difference in my students' lives.
- The work I do matters
- I Love what I do
- There is Power in my Presence
- I will be the best I can be
- I am excited about today
- I will be the best I can be
- I am ready to slay the day

- I am grateful for this adventure and opportunity
- I motivate and empower my students
- I believe in myself and my abilities to lead
- I treat myself and my students with respect and care
- I am a person of high integrity
- I have great purpose in the classroom

Written affirmations are a great way to set intentions for the day ahead. Verbal affirmations work well throughout the day as a nudge when needed—for example, repeating them when feeling overwhelmed at work. Repeating phrases such as "I am the master of my destiny" and "I have endless talents which I can use and share" helps calm negative thoughts. Some days it is challenging to stay positive. Therefore, we must remind ourselves that it is okay to let negative thoughts through sometimes, but not to let them overpower our day. Positive affirmations can become part of our daily routine almost as an aspect of self-care.

CONCLUSION

In summary, we believe adjunct professors should be acknowledged as valuable to our university colleagues because our work is beneficial and necessary. When there is a collaboration between adjunct professors, full-time faculty, and administrators we can achieve the overall mission of the educational institution (Wallin, 2004). The information shared in this chapter echo the sentiments of many in the higher-education community. Such sentiments point out the trials and joys of our lives as adjunct professors. We hope our experiences tell the story of our adversities that have made us feel devalued but also shed light that reminds us that adjunct-land continues to offer us positive opportunities. We know there are many adjunct professors who teach for various reasons, such as the potential to earn optional extra income, a way to spend their retirement years, or simply because they only desire to work a part-time job.

However, we, the authors, and other adjunct professors we know, have experienced deluded hopes that our teaching, service to departments, and drive to go above and beyond our contractual duties would set us on a pathway to transform into full-time faculty. We have applied, interviewed, and watched others get hired in the departments we have worked for years. We have lived with the crazy feeling that the longer we serve as adjunct professors, the more likely we are to remain adjunct professors who are frustrated by the struggle to find a tenure-track position. Therefore, our advice to adjuncts in such situations is to continuously develop a plan to utilize their skills and expertise to solidify a method for obtaining job security. Waiting for colleges and universities to provide this would be the worst fate. Adjunct professors must take responsibility for seeking full-time employment and increasing their earnings when they feel prepared. This process begins with an adjunct understanding of their abilities and value. As adjuncts, we understand that we should seek ways to leverage ourselves and present value in areas that can grow departments. Always set a timeline for how long you will teach at a university and map out your next networking opportunity.

REFERENCES

American Federation of Teachers. (2020). *An army of temps: AFT 2020 adjunct faculty quality of work/life report.* Retrieved from: https://www.aft.org/press-release/ army-temps-report-reveals-grave-plight-contingent-college-faculty

Flaherty, C. (2020, April 20). *Barely getting by.* Inside Higher Ed. https://www.inside highered.com/news/2020/04/20/new-report-says-many-adjuncts-make -less-3500-course-and-25000-year

Wallin, D. L. (2004). Valuing professional colleagues: Adjunct faculty community and technical colleges. *Community College Journal of Research and Practice, 28*(4), 373–391. https://doi.org/10.1080/10668920490424087

Yakoboski, P. J. (2016). Adjunct views of adjunct positions. *Change: The Magazine of Higher Learning, 48*(3), 54–59. https://doi.org/10.1080/00091383.2016.117 0553

PART III

I TEACH BECAUSE I LOVE IT, NOT TO PAY THE BILLS

CHAPTER 10

THROUGH THE LENS OF A "HAVE-NOT"

An Adjunct Faculty's View

Karen Marie Wagner-Clarke

ABSTRACT

Offering insights through the lens of an adjunct faculty member discloses some of the realities of being a "part-time" instructor in higher education. At the collegiate level, a two-tiered faulty system exists that offers greater advantages for full-time or tenure-track faculty and lesser benefits for part-time faculty—adjuncts. The result is marginalized and undervalued adjunct instructors who are paid minimum remuneration and have less collegiate support and services than the full-time or tenure track faculty. Unfortunately, this reality sometimes deters from the purpose—fulfilling a passion for teaching, helping students earn an education while having a positive impact, and making a difference in their academic lives.

There are certain life lessons that you can only learn in the struggle.

—Idowu Koyenikan

Don't Forget About the Adjuncts!, pages 107–118
Copyright © 2023 by Information Age Publishing
www.infoagepub.com
All rights of reproduction in any form reserved.

107

Being an adjunct faculty at a private, nonprofit, nonsectarian, accredited institution has taught me valuable lessons about the challenges and rewards of teaching at the collegiate level. Also, this experience has shed new light on the impact (effect) of the two-tier faculty system in higher education. It is a "bifurcated employment system" which exists and places all full-time or tenure-track faculty in one class, the "haves," and all adjunct faculty in another, the "have-nots" (Gappa & Leslie, 1993, p. 63). Unfortunately, this two-tiered class structure system in academia has become customary. It bestows great prestige and influence on the have while dictating a modicum of privilege and status on the have nots. It reflects a separation of value and underscores disparity. As a result, the adjunct faculty environment discounts our contributions, credentials, competencies, and experiences due to the class structure. Consequently, it leads to the marginalization and devaluation of adjuncts in the academic landscape and neglects the basic employment needs of value, equitable income, benefits, and organizational support. Through an adjunct lens—a have not, I provide critical insights into the adjunct journey, highlight challenges and opportunities posed at the collegiate level, and share some tips/strategies for those contemplating entering the field of higher education. There is also a dose of daily affirmation that keeps me going when the going gets tough. It serves as motivation when I try desperately to charter the, at times, turbulent waters of the adjunct environment.

MY ADJUNCT JOURNEY

Throughout my higher education academic endeavors, I have been deeply and profoundly influenced by some excellent educators (both part- and full-time) who offered much inspiration and support. Those instructors mentored and motivated me and impacted my decision to become a higher-education instructor. Consequently, the desire was to provide the same level of encouragement and support bestowed upon me; so, during my graduate program, I embarked on a teaching journey as part-time faculty—an adjunct.

As an adjunct, I am a part-time academic employee, also known as a contingent instructor, hired to work on a term-by-term basis (Gappa et al., 2005). I am neither considered part of permanent staff nor on a path to a tenured position. Instead, I hold an ad hoc appointment and have conditional employment contingent upon the institution's needs. My schedule is flexible as it varies from semester to semester; it is not constant. It is important to note that as an adjunct, I have never considered moving to full-time faculty ranks, assuming that is even possible. As a "full-mooner"—a part-time faculty member with a full-time job elsewhere—(Gappa & Leslie, 1993;

Tuckman & Pickering, 1988), I am content teaching on a contingency basis and imparting professional experience and industry expertise to students in the classroom environment. My motivation to teach is intrinsic, not extrinsic; money is not the driver. It was not the principal reason for entering part-time teaching. I embarked on the profession because of my passion for teaching, lending knowledge to students, challenging their critical thinking skills, offering insights from the trenches, and pursuing my professional growth and development. Since my journey began approximately 10 years ago, I have facilitated a repertoire of 16 different face-to-face, online, and hybrid courses in four disciplines under four department chairs. My adjunct faculty journey continues today!

WHO ARE THE HAVE-NOTS?

Part-time faculty members, like myself, are an eclectic cohort that brings diversity, energy, passion, dedication, a wide array of education, an extraordinary range of accomplishments, and immense personal circumstances and professional experiences to higher education. Adjuncts are not a monolithic group of marginal employees. On the contrary, we are a heterogeneous population typically well qualified for teaching assignments. We are a rich source to academia as we bring real-world industry experience and expertise to students and collegiate institutions (Caruth & Caruth, 2013). We have varying careers, professional backgrounds, and work histories and are experts, specialists, and professionals in various fields (Gappa & Leslie, 1993; McRae, 2012; Pyram & Roth, 2018). Adjuncts are assets and considered valuable for our "scarce expertise," "teaching performance," and "quality of instruction" offered to students (Gappa & Leslie, 1993, p. 134). Additionally, we provide our academic employers with flexibility and "high levels of productivity and intellectual capital" (Gappa et al., 2005, p. 37). Furthermore, many of us hold terminal degrees in numerous disciplines, have prior teaching experience at other institutions, have full-or part-time positions at other organizations, and some are business owners.

Case in point. I hold multiple master's degrees and a doctorate in education (EdD), possess a Society for Human Resource Management Senior Certified Professional certificate (SHRM-SCP), serve as a technical editor (a capture and proposal services company for government contracts and several textbook publishers), and work as a senior research specialist for a human resource consulting firm. As valuable part-time instructors, adjuncts have many of the same academic responsibilities as full-time or tenure-track faculty.

Case in point. An excerpt from a prestigious private university's part-time faculty handbook below (name intentionally redacted) is shared to expose adjuncts' having the same teaching obligations as full-time or tenure-track faculty. Taken from the "Responsibilities of Adjunct Faculty" section:

> Adjunct faculty must meet the same professional and/or creative standards and requirements as *full-time faculty*, though the principal role of adjunct faculty is to teach, and evidence of teaching ability is a key criterion in the initial selection and continued employment at the University . . . In addition, the expectation is that adjunct faculty will keep *regular office hours*, submit grades in a reasonable and timely manner, and *be available for service* at the university during the term of their employment (empahsis added).

Yet, as adjuncts, marginalization and underappreciation are prevalent, and the reality of disparities exists. It is a fact even though our teaching responsibilities, as highlighted above, mirror our full-time colleagues. Being an adjunct makes me realize that the role is dichotomous and encompasses many compromises against a backdrop of advantages and disadvantages. As a result, the contingent position poses many professional challenges and offers various opportunities that I will highlight.

PERSONAL CHALLENGES FACED

The bifurcated system mentioned earlier is responsible for our—the have-nots—employment conditions and work environments. In the overall scheme of a part-time workforce, we are highly educated and dedicated outliers who deliver a vital core service—education. However, being part-timers, we are undervalued and considered a déclassé faculty despite being highly qualified (Caruth & Caruth, 2013; Gappa et al., 2005; McRae, 2012; Pyram & Roth, 2018). Consequently, we are not deemed as valuable as the haves. As a have not, we earn significantly less pay (payment is a small per-course remuneration), have minimal (if any) health or disability benefits, and get less collegiate support than our full-time or tenured equivalents. While there are numerous challenges, the choice is to highlight the ones most significant in my plight as an adjunct.

Compensation and Benefits

Regarding remuneration, for example, at the university of employ, full-time faculty receive a salary, so regardless of student enrollment, they receive full payment for their assigned courses. On the other hand, as adjuncts, we are paid according to the enrollment numbers. Please note that remuneration is nominal in comparison to full-time faculty. Table 10.1 shows the adjuncts' course payment scale.

TABLE 10.1   Course Payment Scale—Adjuncts

# Enrolled Students	Payment
6+	Full payment (range $2,200.00–$2,600.00)
4–5	2/3 pay
2–3	1/2 pay
1 credit course	1/3 pay
Direct Study (3 credits)	Just over $200.00

As far as health or disability benefits are concerned, there are none! These core employment requirements—employee value, equitable income, and benefits are only for the haves, not the have-nots! This is the reality even though, as mentioned above, the teaching requirements and commitments mirror our full-time or tenure-track counterparts. Fortunately, being employed full time elsewhere and the wife of a U.S. Airforce veteran and Department of Defense employee (40+ years), I neither rely on the discriminatory income nor the health benefits as a part-time employee.

How does this marginalization and devaluation make me feel? Considering I am a valuable contributor to the institution and its academic community, I feel undervalued and under-compensated for my efforts! Please note that I have held the distinction of "exemplary level faculty" since 2018. I was one of the first five faculty and the only adjunct member to receive this status when the program began at the university in Spring 2018. Further, as an adjunct, I hold the same responsibility as the full-time faculty for teaching and ensuring that the university's standards of excellence are met.

Accordingly, I commit the energy and effort needed to ensure the fulfillment of my academic commitment to the institution. Semester after semester, countless hours are dedicated to each course to ensure student success on a continuum. It includes pre-course preparations—reading the course textbook(s), creating assignments, selecting an array of experiential learning tools and resources, crafting/refining/customizing syllabi, loading course(s) information and learning materials in the learning management system, corresponding with the information technology and educational technology departments, and sending notifications to the students—all before the semester begins. Then, there are those scenarios where all pre-course preparations are completed, and a class (or classes) gets canceled at the last minute. It occurs for various reasons, of course!

Last-Minute Cancellations

One semester, my teaching task was three classes for which I had thoroughly prepared. It included committing numerous hours in advance and completing all pre-course preparations, only to have a chair revoke all the teaching assignments two days before the semester began. All the hours dedicated to the pre-course practice are, of course, *ex gratia*. This last-minute cancellation occurred because a full-time faculty member, whom I will call Donna, complained that the courses she favored were assigned to an adjunct—me. Donna did not view classes she desired to facilitate designated to an adjunct as fair considering my part-time status. After all, as a have-not, I am not granted the same value, stature, and respect as a have. Donna also argued that enrollment of several of the same students in the three different classes was evident. Hence, another instructor was best for a "new perspective" and "a change of instruction."

As a note, Donna had taken the time to review my teaching schedule and the name of students enrolled in each class for an entire academic period. So, she was armed with information when launching the complaint to the key administrators and the department chair. Alas, after discussing the last-minute cancellation situation with my chair, she claimed that Donna had much influence and "friends in high places." Consequently, the class cancellation order had come from above, so the chair's hands were tied, and nothing could be done about my removal from the courses.

It is also essential to highlight that many students request my teaching schedule semester after semester. As a result, approximately eight students who formerly attended some of my other courses had intentionally enrolled in these three classes because I was the instructor. Regrettably, they were disappointed that someone other than me—Donna—was the instructor!

Last-Minute Assignments

On the flip side, last-minute assignments are a reality. They can occur for various reasons, so flexibility is the key. That is if the desire is to remain in good graces with the department chairs and continue to receive courses semester-to-semester—a steady part-time gig.

Case in point. One semester, I was contacted by a department chair after a course block had already begun. The request was to facilitate an additional course because another adjunct did not attend the first class session. The 23 students in the class waited for approximately 2 hours for an instructor to no avail. At this time, I will deter from sharing the minute details of what occurred. However, I did accept the task since the chair stated that "I was her last resort" . . . yes, "the last resort," or else cancellation of the class was inevitable since she could not find a substitute instructor, either full- or part-time. Being subjected to class cancellations as an undergraduate, I empathized with the enrolled students. It was my primary reason for agreeing to the task. To that end, there was scant time for preparation. Also, the teaching assignment was at another campus, not where I typically facilitated courses. It was at a campus 2 hours away, one way; that is a 4-hour round trip from my domicile. Since it was an evening course, I decided to stay at a hotel in the area for approximately 8 weeks to spare myself from driving such a long distance late at night and risk falling asleep at the wheel. The hotel charges and gas costs were an out-of-pocket expense, as, even though it was a last-minute teaching request, and "I was the last resort," the university does not cover the expenditures for us have-nots, only the haves! It is vital to highlight that reimbursement of these types of expenses for full-time faculty will likely vary per institution. I do not believe it is a standard practice across the board in higher education.

Collegiate Support and Services

A university requirement is that I hold weekly office hours (2 hours minimum) to meet with students and offer assistance and guidance. However, consulting with students is quite challenging when teaching face-to-face and hybrid courses. Why? There is no official office space allocated for us adjuncts. Therefore, meeting students in the library, cafeteria, vacant classrooms, or campus parking lots are the only options, as offices are only available for full-time faculty (n.b., Online courses are not an issue since meetings with students occur virtually.).

Also, other core services like supplies, tools, mailboxes, telephone, equipment, and other resources, including access to secretarial/administrative support, are minimal. For example, full-time or tenure-track faculty have the administrative staff complete all their copying and preparing tasks for students in advance. However, as a have not, yup, you guessed it . . . many collegiate support and services are unavailable. Consequently, I must arrive at the university, at a minimum, 2 to 3 hours earlier than a scheduled class time to complete those tasks. It is also unpaid hours by the university.

I have learned over the years that, as a have-not, it is best to keep a low profile and not make any waves by speaking up about compensation and benefits, last-minute class cancellations or additions, and lack of collegiate support and services. It is simply best to commit to the task and do what the department chairs and principal administrators expect. If not, it will likely result in not being rehired or assigned another course(s) at the institution. It is important to note that termination or nonrenewal of an adjunct's contract can occur anytime without stating a reason(s). Therefore, keeping in good graces with the department chairs is vital as they control the adjunct environment at the university and make most decisions about the part-time faculty members' overall employment, including initial hiring, rehiring, teaching load, and evaluation.

PERSONAL OPPORTUNITIES REALIZED

Being an adjunct has provided some professional opportunities. First, the university has a professional development program aimed at instructional excellence for all faculty members, including adjuncts. Since I desire to improve my teaching and classroom management skills and become most effective in meeting the students' instructional needs and maintaining the university's standards of excellence, I aggressively embarked on the opportunity to participate in the various workshops. I was, as a result, one of the first five participants to swiftly propel through the program and complete the different stages—essential, proficient, mastery, exemplary—and achieve the ultimate exemplary teaching status (p.s., It looks great on my curriculum vitae!).

Second, there are regular invites to review and provide feedback on textbooks from higher-education publishers like McGraw-Hill, Pearson, Cengage, and Flatworld. Perquisites often received with the solicitations are access to e-textbooks, hard copies, and additional instructional academic tools and resources. Another is invitations to seminars, webinars, and other educational workshops to increase collegiate knowledge, skills, and aptitudes (KSAs). These offers have evolved into an opportunity to become a technical editor (1099-contract employment) for McGraw-Hill and a Proposal Management Company (government contractors).

Third, due to my faculty status, I am frequently requested by colleagues and acquaintances alike to give presentations to students and employees. For the past few years, I have been giving semi-annual presentations to graduate students at Georgetown University–College of Continuing Studies–Human Resource Management program. Also, invitations are regularly extended to provide leadership and human resource management advice to employees at various organizations, for-profit, not-for-profit, public, and private entities.

STRATEGIES FOR THOSE ANTICIPATING
THE ADJUNCT FACULTY ENVIRONMENT

Below are some practical techniques to navigate the collegiate environment and maintain my contingency appointment.

Strategy 1

Conducting due diligence and thoroughly investigating the collegiate institution. It includes assessing the organization's remuneration policies, reading the adjunct faculty handbook, and reviewing part-time facilitators' employment practices and protocols. Knowing the remuneration before committing to a contingency appointment and teaching assignments is essential. Why? Because having foreknowledge will ensure that, if the effort is extrinsically motivated, that is, teaching at the collegiate level is based on an economic motive, the need will be satisfied. Also, it will mitigate any misconceptions regarding the institution's compensation strategy. Also, education on the employment practices and policies will deter false beliefs or expectations in the adjunct environment. As the adage goes, knowledge is the key to success!

Strategy 2

Networking with peers and linking to one or more advocates who work full-time at the institution. It includes accepting invitations to peer networking activities—both internal and external of the institution's environment. For example, I often attend networking and other social events offered by my colleagues who work full-time at the university or are adjuncts, like myself, and extend invitations to their corporate events. It is a crucial strategy as relationships, assimilation, and integration are core to the collegiate landscape.

Strategy 3

Building a good relationship with academic deans, chairs, and administrators. It is the ticket to becoming a part of the "in-group." Once a chair or dean favors an adjunct faculty, the individual becomes a part of the in-group and receives the maximum allocated courses for the semester. Becoming and remaining a part of the favored team of part-timers has its benefits. However, realistically, it is a challenge as membership requires (a) ongoing commitment to the department, (b) doing what is required precisely without pause or question(s), (c) completing particular tasks and projects (often without pay), and (d) accepting last-minute teaching assignments without hesitation (p.s., I have made it to the ranks of the in-group and, to date, have a steady flow of teaching assignments.).

Strategy 4

Being flexible. Flexibility is essential because classes will be added, revoked, or canceled at the last minute. As shared prior, there is also the possibility of late-minute assignments with scant preparation time. Further, there are no guarantees for year-round assignments, as courses and schedules depend on student enrollment levels. Finally, flexibility correlates to having a financial plan, as in the adjunct environment, there is no financial security as remuneration is minimal, and there is no guaranteed teaching schedule.

Strategy 5

Having a financial plan. It is vital as an adjunct, if possible, to have other sources of income or other forms of financial reliability. An adjunct's pay per course is minimal, and the schedule is unreliable. For example, at the university, adjunct teaching assignments are limited to 10 classes per annum; however, many part-time faculty hardly get assigned that many classes per year. The reality is approximately six courses per year—two classes per semester or course block. Further, the number of students enrolled in a class (depending on the institution) determines the pay, as revealed earlier. Income is unreliable; therefore, having a financial plan is crucial in the adjunct environment.

Strategy 6

Keeping a low profile and committing to the task of teaching and engaging with students. It is best if the desire is to keep in the good graces of full-time faculty and administrators and get rehired semester after semester. It includes accepting that there will be significant out-of-class preparation and meeting with students outside regular class hours and often without a designated office space. A suggestion for out-of-class preparation, pre-and post-course, is to allocate an hour or two daily to academic tasks. Having a routine lightens the load and mitigates trying to get all the teaching requirements completed at the last minute. Performing required duties at crunch time successfully never work and is highly stressful. The same goes for meeting with students. Scheduling weekly sessions post-class in a designated space such as the library or an empty classroom (or in the same course classroom if available) provides an expectation and routine for students and yourself.

WORDS OF AFFIRMATION USED TO NAVIGATE THE TURBULENT WATERS OF THE HAVE-NOTS

Being an adjunct, as stated prior, has its rewards and challenges. Unfortunately, at times, the benefits are few and the challenges are plenty. So, it is vital to have an affirmation to navigate the sometimes-turbulent waters of the have-nots!

A daily affirmation used throughout my interactions to keep me going through the challenges is the chorus of the song "Three Little Birds" by Bob Marley (1977). Since childhood, I have listened to this reggae tune and followed the words: "Don't worry about a thing, 'cause every little thing gonna be all right." This chorus resonates and offers solace when I navigate the turbulent waters as a have-not! Such simple yet profound words offer positive affirmations to combat my subconscious patterns and replace them with more adaptive narratives. The rhetoric taps into my unconscious mind and serves as motivation; it reverses any negative thinking patterns and replaces them with positive thoughts. This self-affirmation has helped me overcome many challenges during my adjunct plight. When I am highly stressed about the adjunct environment with its marginalization and devaluation conditions, I hum the tune over and over again.

> Rise up this morning
> Smiled with the rising sun
> Three little birds pitch by my doorstep
> Singing sweet songs of melodies pure and true
> Saying, this is my message to you
> Singing, don't worry about a thing
> 'Cause every little thing gonna be all right (Marley, 1977)

It reaffirms that the current situation or challenge faced is only temporary. As the Persian adage goes, "This too shall pass." Further, with purpose and perseverance, *everything* will *be all right* in the long term!

IN SUMMARY

The experience viewed through the lens of a have-not provided some insights and hopefully shed some light on both the positive and negative aspects of being an adjunct at the collegiate level. The two-tiered employment system of the haves and the have-nots poses challenges and promotes unfavorable employment conditions—marginalization and devaluation of adjuncts. As contingency employees, unfortunately, we are not extended the same prestige and privilege as our full-time or tenure-track colleagues. As highlighted in the narrative, there have been some challenges in my adjunct journey, including a transient course schedule, nominal remuneration, and minimal collegiate support and services. The said issues, among others, require the employment of a daily affirmation to keep me motivated and help me navigate a turbulent adjunct environment. However, regardless of the drawbacks, my teaching motivation is intrinsic and has been and continues to be student-centered. My purpose of helping students earn an education remains steadfast, and my passion for teaching remains intact. So, I believe I am fulfilling my primary goal of teaching in higher education, supporting students on their educational journey, making a difference in the classroom, and promoting their academic success on a continuum. My adjunct journey in higher education continues!

REFERENCES

Caruth, G. D., & Caruth, D. L. (2013). Adjunct faculty: Who are these unsung heroes of academe? *Current Issues in Education, 16*(3), 1–11. Retrieved June 23, 2022 from https://cie.asu.edu/ojs/index.php/cieatasu/article/view/1269/528

Gappa, J. M., Austin, A. E., & Trice, A. G. (2005). Rethinking academic work and workplaces. *Change: The Magazine of Higher Learning, 37*(6), 32–39. https://doi.org/10.3200/CHNG.37.6.32-39

Gappa, J. M., & Leslie, D. W. (1993). *The invisible faculty: Improving the status of part-timers in higher education.* Jossey-Bass.

Marley, B. (1977). *Three Little Birds* [Video]. https://www.youtube.com/watch?v=ind7BEZgWJU

McRae, L. (2012). The exploitation of expertise: Adjunct academics and the commodification of knowledge. *Fast Capitalism, 9*(1), 89–97. https://fastcapitalism.journal.library.uta.edu/index.php/fastcapitalism/article/view/268/310

Pyram, M. J., & Roth, S. I. (2018). For-profit career college adjunct faculty and their affiliation needs and experiences. *Research in Higher Education Journal, 34*, 1–11. https://files.eric.ed.gov/fulltext/EJ1178403.pdf

Tuckman, H. P., & Pickerill, K. L. (1988). Part-time faculty and part-time academic careers. In D. E. Breneman & T. Youn (Eds), *Academic labor markets and careers* (pp. 98–113). The Falmer Press.

CHAPTER 11

THE UNSUNG HERO

Loubert Senatus

ABSTRACT

This chapter submission details an adjunct member's experience in a community college setting. As part-time employees, adjuncts are the gap fillers to the college engine. There are many conversations about adjuncts' roles in the higher education learning system. This chapter adds to the ongoing collection of adjunct members' experiences in the community college system.

I have the pleasure of serving in one of the largest community college systems in the country. I have been teaching for the last 6 years approaching 7 from the time I write this submission. I teach in the social sciences department at the college. There are four courses I customarily teach, depending on the need of that particular semester. The four classes are Sociology, Intro to Social Science, Social Problems, and Student Survival Skills (the first year experience course), designed for students in a reading or math developmental course. I love teaching college students, especially in community college institutions, because that is where the population of students that I am most passionate about end up enrolling. One major challenge facing community college leaders is the college completion agenda

Don't Forget About the Adjuncts!, pages 119–124
Copyright © 2023 by Information Age Publishing
www.infoagepub.com
All rights of reproduction in any form reserved.

119

(Goldrick-Rab, 2018). The research indicates that it is hard for students to complete their degrees, so serving as an adjunct professor is my contribution to witnessing students succeed in college. On average, only 4 out of 10 students I meet will end up completing college (Elfman, 2020). My passion for seeing students win informs how I approach the profession and what makes serving as an adjunct one of the unique roles in higher education.

CHALLENGES

A myriad of challenges of being an adjunct is that the scheduling of courses is not always favorable, so each adjunct requires a continual adjustment by the semester. Planning and balancing other obligations with full-time work and familial obligations makes it hard to do so if you want to remain in the reliable adjunct pool. At a minimum, adjunct professors have to be comfortable being assigned the courses that the full-time faculty do not want to teach, in terms of time offerings which could include weekend and evening courses. Essentially, adjunct professionals are offered the courses from the remaining menu of available sections. That could challenge the adjunct professional who wants consistent work with college students in the classroom.

Additionally, adjunct faculty are at the mercy of enrollment—which means that the adjunct courses are the first to be canceled if there are not enough students enrolled in a course. It is challenging to feel like you are an essential part of the academic department, especially for new adjuncts working in colleges with a large student population. The feelings of professional isolation arise as you try to foster relationships with full-time faculty. As an adjunct, I feel I am there to fill a void but not included in the larger mission of providing opportunities to enrich the lives of individuals in our community. Adjunct faculties are the unseen and unsung heroes of academic departments who feel institutionally isolated. My evidence for that comes from my experience of trying to establish relationships with full-time faculty.

In my first year of teaching, I had to develop my course syllabus for one of the courses I was excited to teach. As a new hire, I knew no one else teaching the curriculum, so there was no one I could turn to for suggestions or feeling like I was heading the right way. I tried emailing a few in the department, but my emails were not replied to in time for me to feel secure about the course syllabus. The anxiety of showing up as prepared was insurmountable. I did not feel that much pressure in my full-time job. I would have benefitted from some mentorship, but as an adjunct (and it could be me not understanding the infrastructure), I often feel isolated from full-time faculty.

Trying to get technical support was challenging as well for the textbook. I had to contact the book publisher to gain some support on accessing the

The Unsung Hero • **121**

technology that I knew would be a resource to help my teaching job feel manageable. What made it even more challenging one semester was that I ended up being assigned to the same course at two different campuses. Unbeknownst to me, the difference in campuses meant that the department chair selected different textbooks for the same course. I think this situation was unique because I was (from my knowledge) the only adjunct teaching the same course at two separate campuses for the same institution. It was adding to my feeling of isolation on the campus. There is a distance between the adjunct faculty and the department chair after you are hired to teach. The closest I got to my department chair was fostering a colleague-ship with the department secretary (or assistant), which proved worthwhile. The assistants on each of the campuses I worked at ended up being a life-line on many occasions when I felt lost in the weeds of the department.

Another challenge as an adjunct is the limitations around chairing organizations or extracurricular clubs at the college. Some clubs pique my interest, especially Phi Theta Kappa, which has a similar vision and mission to what I do in my full-time job. I love being of service to students and coaching them up to their fullest potential, but as an adjunct faculty, I am limited in my involvement because I am not a full-time employee. Institutionally, adjuncts are not invited to chair those organizations, although they are not discouraged either; it is just a peculiar situation to live in when as an employee, you feel stuck in the middle of an unexplained process. In one case, I felt discontentment because some of my former high school students enrolled in the club because of my advice about becoming involved at the college. I was invested in their growth because I met some of those students in my full-time capacity at their previous high school. I wanted a continuum of coaching them up to survive the college landscape, but I was limited because of my status as an adjunct. As an adjunct, there is rarely a forum to express your discontent about existing structures. The solution is to try to increase your visibility at the college.

An additional challenge of being an adjunct is not receiving the nod for national professional development opportunities. It could be disheartening for adjuncts that have served in the reliable adjunct pool for over 6 years. There are adjuncts with aspirations of playing a more prominent role in community college administration; however, the opportunities are limited to full-time faculty or higher. One requirement to attend national professional developments is that the college's representative is a full-time hire. The ceiling is capped to the classroom for adjuncts, contributing to my sense of isolation at the college. Adjuncts are not granted the same provision as full-time employees—to some degree; I understand why that is the case (from an administrative standpoint). However, adjuncts that have consistently served for over 5 years or more are a value-add to the college that often goes unnoticed. I would like a chance to be part of those national professional developments and be sponsored by longstanding and outstanding adjunct faculty.

The last challenge I want to share about adjuncts' journey in community colleges, especially long-serving adjuncts, is that there is no process where job security is at play for that position. In my state, some organizers are planning to unionize for adjunct faculty to increase salary; however, that never was my standpoint. I would have loved a process similar to the full-time faculty of a tenure track. As a recurring theme in this chapter, there are systemic issues with adjunct faculty being classified as part time that does not grant certain perquisites as tenured faculty is limited to full-time faculty. I understand that the budget is a priority for department chairs and presidents; however, some standing that acknowledges the adjunct's value to the institution, insomuch as that they maintain a priority hire status for the department, would speak volumes for adjunct professionals.

OPPORTUNITIES

The opportunity afforded me as an adjunct is the institutional professional development series. The slate of courses to build one's skill set at the college is endless. For instance, a couple of courses enriched my skill set as an instructor at the college. One was a course on effective college instruction that partnered with the Association of College and University Educators. I was able to build a rapport with participants from my institution alongside other colleagues all over the country. The institution opened the opportunity specifically for adjuncts. When the opportunity was passed on to the adjunct professionals, I took advantage of the opportunity to learn and build my skill set and walked away from the course with newfound practices that enhanced my teaching style. I continually searched the course menu and enrolled in as many courses as my time could manage. The two courses I recently completed were Inclusive Teaching for Equitable Learning and Applying the Quality Matters Rubric. Those two courses provided the necessary enrichment I needed to adapt to online learning and provide an inclusive environment for all students during the pandemic.

I find it essential to continually build on your teaching approach when working in the college because the teaching landscape constantly evolves. In addition to the landscape, the learning management systems fluctuate every so often, so staying ahead of the learning limits the anxieties of trying to learn something before you teach a course to students on utilizing the learning management systems. In order to maximize the technological aspects of teaching, you must be committed to learning the technology. I was initially resistant and was comfortable with my old-school approach of using the whiteboard, PowerPoint slides, and good ole fashion to facilitate excellent Socratic conversations in the classroom. However, the pandemic forced me to shift to this generation's new way of learning. I am better because of the college's institutional and professional development.

STRATEGIES FOR ENTERING THE ADJUNCT PROFESSION

A strategy that I find successful is knowing your discipline. It may sound strange considering that the assumption is that you are already being hired because you know your discipline. However, I find that being confident about your subject benefits students in the classroom. I teach in the social sciences, so in our everyday discourse, there will be varying thoughts and perspectives that can contradict one's beliefs. Nevertheless, when you are well-versed in your subject, you can create episodes of enlightenment for all students in the classroom. For example, I had one student that vehemently believed that racism did not exist. If I had responded emotionally, the class would have missed the learning opportunity. However, I was able to teach over the next few weeks through different modules, exercises, and reading assignments that brought this student to the revelation that racism does exist in our society. In short, adjuncts must be confident in their teaching subject regardless of how often they teach. The advice here is never to stop learning in your field.

Another strategy is to build relationships with the assistant to the department chair. Many professionals overlook the proverbial "helpers," but the truth is that they know where all the keys to the buildings are and are in control of scheduling. It is because of my tone in my emails, the sending of the cards to let them know that I appreciate them, that I am often one of the department's favorites, and often consulted with after full-time workers select the courses. In some instances, I was asked what classes I preferred.

Find ways to be involved on campus. The only way for people to know you is for people to see you. Volunteering on committees and showing up to social events on campus is essential. The administration personnel are always at committee-sponsored events. The more familiar you are with administration, the more professional growth opportunities are present. However, do not join committees for advancement at the institution; join committees because you are passionate about the committee you seek and want to learn more about the intricacies involved with that committee and its impact on the institution.

AFFIRMATIONS

An affirmation that means the most to me is "it is what it is because it will never be what it is not." A practice that I use in my everyday life is to take seven. Seven is a significant number to me for various reasons. I meditate for 7 minutes in my car before walking into my classroom. The first 7 minutes upon each wakening of my day, I give myself 7 minutes to be present with myself. I learned how to take seven during my short time living in the pacific northwest. In short, each minute, I honor one of the teachings of the seven grandfathers (humility, bravery, honesty, wisdom, truth, respect, and love). This practice centers my thoughts and intentions as I get ready to connect with my students. The second source of motivation is looking at my newborn son—I have a picture of him and my dad as my screensaver. I can see his eyes. Every time I look in Selah's eyes, I am reminded of the promise I made to him while watching him come into this world. To "have his back" means that I need to develop him into a lifelong learner and continually answer his curiosities about the world. I see my students with that same lens. The affirmation is that I am because you are. Reminding and repeating that affirmation supports the mission of seeing my students win in the classroom so they can be what they need for their families.

CLOSING THOUGHTS

I want aspiring adjunct professionals to know the profession's good, bad, and indifferent perspectives. As an adjunct working in one of the country's largest community colleges, I carry a perspective of what the realities are and what my experience has been. It is also essential to know that every adjunct instructor will have their own set of experiences that makes the position unique and nuanced to the discipline they teach. Regardless of what you teach, the profession requires much commitment to serving adults trying to make their way in this world. It is a special calling and an extraordinary void that we are filling serving as adjunct instructors. It is much akin to a yeoman's work. It is a position that does not come filled with much praise. Sometimes you are simply a number, a contractor, or a vendor there to do a job—but it is an important one. As for front-facing warriors for the institution, we often become the lifeline to whether a student persists through their studies—and that is a responsibility worthy of the unsung heroes.

REFERENCES

Elfman, L. (2020, April 2). A completion agenda. *Diverse: Issues in Higher Education*, 20–21. https://www.diverseeducation.com

Goldrick-Rab, S. (2018, December 3). Addressing community college completion rates by securing students' basic needs. *New Directions for Community Colleges*, 184, 7–16. https://doi.org/10.1002/cc.20323

CHAPTER 12

LIFE ON THE BUBBLE

Shelagh Smith

ABSTRACT

Life on the Bubble discusses my experiences teaching at multiple academic institutions for nearly 20 years. It covers the pitfalls, as well as the benefits, of teaching up to eight classes per semester as an adjunct faculty member. Life on the Bubble examines the different requirements and expectations of these institutions and how to navigate them.

BACKGROUND

I've been an adjunct faculty member at multiple institutions, including University of Massachusetts, Bridgewater State University, Massachusetts Maritime Academy, and Stonehill College. My teaching career began as a teaching assistant in graduate school in 2004 and I've been teaching consistently across multiple organizations since then.

Don't Forget About the Adjuncts!, pages 125–132
Copyright © 2023 by Information Age Publishing
www.infoagepub.com
All rights of reproduction in any form reserved.

125

CHALLENGES

We strive for excellence at this institution, but we temper that with the need to care *genuinely* for each student. With that in mind, we need you to be more nurturing. Students—and their parents—expect teachers, especially *female* teachers, to be more motherlike. Can you do that? (Liberal Arts College. Tuition: $46K per year)

We are dealing with a very diverse group of students whose skills may not be as good as they could be, but we also have a retention problem, and you know that administration doesn't like that. Aim for a lot of B's in your class. B+ if possible. More B's. You get what I'm saying? (State University. Tuition: $15K per year)

This is a regimental academy. We take their work seriously. These students do more than you do each day before you even get out of bed. If they fall asleep in class, wake them. If they don't come to class, file an honor violation. (Regimental Academy. Tuition: $12K per year)

These are just some of the discussions I've had over the years with various faculty and administration members at some of the institutions in which I've taught—simultaneously. Balancing the varying needs of administration, couched in the myth that it's "all for the students' benefit," can be an experience fraught with peril. One misstep and you run the risk of not being invited back to teach next semester. I've seen more than one adjunct faculty new hire not make a second semester due to some violation of the sometimes unspoken code of conduct for adjuncts. The emotional toll can sometimes be overwhelming, but then there are the tangible challenges as well.

As you prepare for each semester in each setting, you must create multiple syllabi. Sometimes you're fortunate enough to teach the same course across more than one school; sometimes you're teaching two or three different courses at each school (each requiring different prep and different syllabi). But if you teach the same course at another school, you must make sure to change all of the institution names, lest a parent see the same syllabus with another school's name on it, a school considered to be lesser quality, and demand answers from administration. (And yes, that's happened to a coworker.) Much soothing was required of the parent, because they, like their children, don't realize that upwards of 70% of college classes are taught by adjuncts (Young & Townsend, 2021).) An email warning was directed to the part-time faculty contingent, creating yet another wave of anxiety, coupled with frustration. Studies have shown that approximately 25% of adjuncts rely on public assistance programs, teaching at multiple colleges, and still they struggle to make ends meet (Flaherty, 2020). If adjuncts don't teach at multiple colleges, often they simply won't earn enough to meet basic needs.

So, each semester creates its own pitfalls because you live in a constant state of anxiety, and the questions that race through your mind can be nerve wracking:

- What is this school's attendance policy? Am I allowed to even have one?
- Is there a cutoff for a "passing" grade? Does this school give credit for Ds? Or only Cs?
- Who is the chairperson this year? Am I going to have yet another classroom evaluation?
- What if I get sick? Will I be covered by this school's part-time faculty sick policy?
- How do I balance my teaching style to meet the needs of each institution?

What if your polices are too harsh at one school, but not strict enough at another? How do you walk that tightrope? What if one college demands masking and COVID-19 precautions, but another doesn't? What are their policies on remote teaching? And what is the approach of one chairperson versus another when it comes to evaluations?

One evaluator may adopt a lecture style, rather than a classroom discussion mode, or vice versa. How do you navigate that kind of code-switching? It is a constant balancing act which can require as much forethought and planning as classroom lectures do, so the best advice would be to observe the environment, reach out to other adjunct faculty, and cautiously test the waters by co-writing assignments, attending orientations, and asking for help or advice if you are ever unsure about anything. Transparency around their expectations is key.

And then, at the end of the semester, a new set of questions will appear to fret over:

- If I grade too harshly, will I get another class?
- If I grade too leniently, will I get another class?
- What will my evaluations say?
- What will my students say on Rate My Professor if I'm not "motherly" enough, if I'm too "soft" for one institution, if my grades are too low for yet another?
- Will those ratings factor into my chair's decision to rehire me next semester?
- Did I adjust my teaching style to meet the needs of each audience enough to meet the requirements of administration?

Ideally, you'll be evaluated by students each semester and will have a good understanding of how you did, but there are other ways to avoid any surprises. The best technique is to adopt transparency with the students as much as with the department administration. Check in often with students to gauge their involvement, interest, and their perceptions on how they—and you—are doing. This will allow for any "on-the-fly" adjustments as the semester moves along because there are few things worse than receiving negative student evaluations at the end of the semester, especially if the chairperson is particularly unforgiving. Plus, it benefits you to never forget that there is a waiting list of adjuncts behind you, all willing to take your classes at the drop of a hat.

Teaching style is incredibly important, especially in an era where students often view themselves as consumers and can adopt the "customer is always right" attitude. It's important we change our approach to meet their needs, depending upon the environment. For example, at the regimental academy, students were upset some restrictions were reduced across the board—they were actually disappointed that they were no longer allowed to be "dropped," meaning they could be required to "drop and give me 20" pushups for a transgression! They reminded me frequently that the academy was regimental and they were "supposed to get toughened up." Conversely, at a tiny liberal arts college, extensions for late work or accommodations for other transgressions were encouraged. "Adopt a more lenient attendance policy, these kids are struggling," one might hear.

Of course, we should always want our teaching styles to match the needs of the students, but when you live (and teach) on the "bubble," then it might not necessarily matter what *your* inherent teaching style or philosophy is; your goal shifts to meeting the needs of each individual department and the everchanging chairpersons because getting another class becomes vitally important in a career where you have absolutely no expectation of guaranteed employment from one semester to another.

Ideally, the teaching style of the chairperson and your style will align, but at the end of the day, it is really about meeting the needs of the students. They are, ultimately, the ones who matter most.

BENEFITS

For me, this career path (if it can be called that, because there is no actual *path* for adjuncts) has been invaluable in terms of flexibility. The sleepless nights worrying over money and health benefits are nowhere near as stressful as having to worry about balancing a 40-hour a week job with a soul-crushing commute while struggling to care for an ill parent, ill siblings, or any of the cruel events life will throw at you. But this path is not for everyone.

Honestly, I never thought it would be for *me*. And yet, here I am. And while I would love to say I had more security and more support by having a full-time contract or full-time position, I know I would miss the frenetic pace too much.

OPPORTUNITY

By taking the adjunct route and opting to remain on the bubble, I've had an amazing amount of opportunity. Have I had to forego a lot of personal scholarship? Absolutely. But, at the same time, I've had the opportunity to work with an amazing array of professionals across many organizations, and I have taught people I would never have imagined teaching, like a former Red Sox pitcher, and the Boston Marathon bomber. (That's a whole other story!)

In any given year, while working for a regimental academy, I have the opportunity to see students come into classes at the beginning of a semester and literally sail off on "sea term" to see the world after only 15 short weeks. I am encouraged and inspired by their bravery and determination, especially of the cadre of young women pursuing a career in such typically masculine fields like marine engineering, or maritime operations. I often tell these students that if I could do it all over again, I would choose their school, their major, and explore the path not taken.

While working for a tiny liberal arts college, I had the opportunity to see how the "other half" lives. I saw students come to class with their Coach bags, pulling up in their BMW convertibles, only to find out later that these students of privilege had many of the same issues their counterparts faced at other institutions. They struggled with mental health issues, they fretted over grades, they broke up and made up with their college sweethearts. The only difference was they had a softer place to fall. If an assignment came in late or if they found themselves struggling, it was expected that there would be no penalty so significant it would impact their overall grade and standing. Supporting and nurturing students was the norm, and it taught me that no assignment due date was as important as an individual's mental health and security.

And while working for a diverse state-run institution, I see students whose experiences mirror my own. They are first-generation college students. Many are paralyzed by imposter syndrome. They're seeking their path, much as I sought my own, and they make the same mistakes I made, with nowhere to fall but back on their own grit to do more with what they've been given. So, for those experiences, and for forging relationships with other faculty and students, I am eternally grateful. I say this to anyone who asks why I do it: Because the students make me laugh, every single day. And they give me hope for the future.

STRATEGIES FOR SURVIVING THE BUBBLE

Now, being hopeful and inspired is one thing, but that's not to say that there are not pitfalls when working with diverse groups of students across multiple institutions while trying to balance my own messy life on scatter-shot paychecks. There is no guaranteed expectation of employment, so there is no way to determine how much money I might make each year. That vacation to Turks and Caicos? Maybe next year. *Hard* maybe. What, we need a new roof? Better start saving now and hope we don't need a new furnace, too! But frankly, the financial pitfalls are secondary to the other challenges that come our way.

Administration—and more importantly their view of the adjunct pool— is probably the biggest challenge. I outlasted a change in administration that decided, quite arbitrarily it seemed, to do away with the adjunct pool in place because the majority of us had only masters degrees, and not doctorates. No matter that most of the masters degrees came from that very university! And let's not forget that most newly minted PhDs don't want to teach freshmen composition classes. But still, that was the administration's decision, and the herd was culled. The sense of betrayal was palpable among the part-time faculty contingent, made worse when we realized we were still paying off student loans to that very institution. But, as adjuncts, we were absolutely powerless to do anything about it as the bubble popped beneath us. We simply packed our bags and moved on to the next school, added our names to the list of next-in-line adjuncts, and hoped for the best.

And then, of course, there are the departmental politics that can wreak havoc on the adjunct pool. Having once been told a class I was scheduled for was cut to give "new adjunct faculty classes" mystified me, until I realized there were romantic entanglements and friendships between administration, higher level institution employees, and the newcomers. Even with a stack of positive student evaluations and a long history with the institution, it mattered not one bit. When pressed about why I had lost a class, I was told I was "a very valuable member of the department," and yet there was nothing that could be done. I suppose that could happen anywhere and I tried to take it in stride, but the bitter taste it left in my mouth lingers to this day.

Finally, and not without merit, there's your own teaching style to consider. Reflecting back on the institution that said I needed to be more "motherly," I needed to adjust my approach to students. I found that they preferred less direct comments on their work, and the vast majority of those comments had better be positive in nature! (Whether or not I saw any change in their skills is a different issue.)

So how do you navigate these challenges?

First, be flexible. Realize early and often that you have virtually no control over what happens to you on the adjunct path. You can apply for jobs,

Life on the Bubble • **131**

you can get classes, but there is no guarantee you'll ever get another. So be flexible in your approach and mindset.

Second, remember that favorite break-up saying "It's not you, it's me"? Well, in the case of adjuncting, it's *really not you*. It's likely them. Adjuncts are subject to the whims of administration. You can be the best teacher the department has, with the highest student ratings, but if you're at the top of the pay scale and they need to cut costs, you're gone. And they never have to say that to you; they can simply say, "We don't have any classes for you this semester." Does that mean you're a failure? No, of course not. It just means that there are a lot of things beyond our control. So remember that phrase: "It's really not you."

Make your presence known on campus. Join committees, and yes, the idea of free work is not a pleasant one, but remember, too, why you're there. Are you there to help students learn? Then join a committee geared to students. Volunteer for additional duties if you feel they would benefit you or your students. Remember, institutions are geared toward expanding the vision of the students; why, then, shouldn't we expand our vision too? And by doing more on campus, you're forging stronger relationships, meeting great people, and expanding your CV as well!

And finally, familiarize yourself with your options. Know your rights—as many as you may have. If you can join a union, join that union. Not all unions are great, but not being in one is worse. Know what the contract says. Know what the union will do for you, how classes are assigned (if covered by the contract), how pay is calculated, what your obligations are in terms of class time, what you're allowed to do (freedom of teaching clauses, etc.). Knowledge is power.

GETTING THROUGH IT ALL

It's easy to get discouraged as an adjunct faculty member. Overall, I feel adjunct faculty are less valued than they should be. It was enlightening to me, years ago, when a tenured professor in my department pulled me aside and said, "Thank you for what you do. You not only teach the courses we don't want to teach, you teach the students the things they need to know to be successful when they get into our classes."

Those words—that simple expression of appreciation—meant the world to me then, and still do today. Adjuncts live on the bubble; we are always under pressure, working for lower wages, often without health benefits, retirement accounts, or any semblance of job security. We are often excluded from departmental decisions, from the rewards that come with a full-time faculty or tenure track positions, but we do the hard work the students need us to do.

And that, in a nutshell, is why I do it.

I don't do it for money—God knows there's never enough of that for adjuncts. I don't do it for praise.

I do it because the students need us—the adjuncts are often the front lines, teaching the classes the tenured profs don't want to teach. They need us to help them be successful, and when they send that email later on in their college career (or even after graduation) asking you a question, or seeking a reference, you can finally see you've made a difference in their lives.

Takeaways

Now you may ask, is adjuncting for you? Maybe. Maybe not.

I hope, from reading this chapter, that you have a clearer understanding of some of the challenges and some of the rewards.

But ask yourself the most important question of all: "Why am I doing this? Do I love what I do?"

If you know why you're doing it (for an income, no matter how shaky that might be), for rewards (few and far between), or because you love teaching (and there's a lot to love about it!), then making the decision to embark on an adjuncting career or to stay in that current role will be an easy one.

REFERENCES

Flaherty, C. (2020, April 20). *Barely getting by.* Inside Higher Ed. https://www.insidehighered.com/news/2020/04/20/new-report-says-many-adjuncts-make-less-3500-course-and-25000-year

Young, J. C., & Townsend, R. B. (2021, August 30). The adjunct problem is a data problem. *The Chronicle of Higher Education.* https://www.chronicle.com/article/the-adjunct-problem-is-a-data-problem?bc_nonce=0y6c76nbg2de3z9d5rlaj&cid=reg_wall_signup

ABOUT THE EDITOR

Antione D. Tomlin, PhD, PCC, is an associate professor and department chair of Academic Literacies at Anne Arundel Community College. He earned his PhD in language, literacy and culture from the University of Maryland, Baltimore County, his MA in higher education administration with a specialization in student affairs from Morgan State University, and his BS in psychology from Stevenson University. Antione is also an ICF-trained and certified life coach.

Don't Forget About the Adjuncts!, page 133
Copyright © 2023 by Information Age Publishing
www.infoagepub.com
All rights of reproduction in any form reserved.

ABOUT THE CONTRIBUTORS

Leslie Ekpe, is pursuing a PhD at TCU in higher educational leadership and is president of the TCU Graduate Student Association. Ekpe also serves as the vice president of the American Association of Colleges for Teacher Education (AACTE) Holmes Program. Ekpe is an alumna of Alabama A&M University, where she earned her bachelor's degree in management, and the University of Alabama at Birmingham, where she obtained her Master of Arts in communication management. She also holds an MBA from Sam Houston State University. Ekpe is a former professional communications teacher for Uplift Education Public Charter School Network. Her research seeks to promote access for marginalized students at the postsecondary level, with a specific focus on college access policies, racial politics in education, and affirmative action policies in higher education.

Ashlee Daniels, is a doctoral student at Prairie View A&M University studying to receive her degree in educational leadership. She serves as a lecturer in the Languages and Communications Department at Prairie View A&M University. Her research focuses on how to best accommodate Black women in higher education through the lens of Edenism, a theoretical framework that she created as a solution for best critical thinking teaching practices and strategies for children of color. Her work is guided by Edenism to provide mentorship and support for Black female students matriculating through college and to prepare them for successful career positions. Ashlee's research interests include the effects of diversity on college campuses, Black female leadership, the curricular implementation for students of color, and

---

Don't Forget About the Adjuncts!, pages 135–140
Copyright © 2023 by Information Age Publishing
www.infoagepub.com
All rights of reproduction in any form reserved.

136 ▪ About the Contributors

the articulation and the manifestation of critical thinking skills by students of color at predominantly White institutions (PWIs) and HBCUs.

Raleta S. Dawkins, PhD, is an adjunct instructor in the Educator Preparation and the Family and Consumer Sciences Departments at NCAT. She is a recent graduate of Old Dominion University. She is a Greensboro, NC native and enjoys spending time with her little one, Dakota Greysen, and husband, Kyle. Raleta earned a Doctor of Philosophy in early childhood education in 2020 from Old Dominion University; a Master of Arts in education, elementary education in 2008 from North Carolina Agricultural & Technical State University, and a Bachelor of Science in elementary education from NCAT in 2004. Her educational aspirations revolve around helping diverse individuals prepare for occupations defined by excellence and grounded in improving educational institutions and society.

Saleena Frazier, EdD, is a proud native of Winston-Salem, NC. She graduated in 1996 from The University of North Carolina at Greensboro with a Bachelors of Science in business administration. She later graduated in 2003, with a master's in information and technology management. While in Charlotte, NC, she worked as assistant vice president within the Financial Banking Industry until 2009 in the information and technology field, while working as an adjunct professor for The University of Phoenix and ITT Technical Institute. Dr. Frazier returned to Forsyth County in 2009 where she reconnected through participating as a member of Jack and Jill of America, Inc. and Alpha Kappa Alpha Sorority, Inc. In 2019, she graduated with her doctorate in organizational leadership from Grand Canyon University. She now owns and operates a community-based childcare facility with a mission dedicated to fostering early childhood preparedness through offering culturally responsive child development. She encourages the use and accessibility of resources within the community for children and works closely with community partners to create a model of service that is needs-led, rather than built around professional boundaries.

Sylviane Ngandu-Kalenga Greensword, graduated with a Master of Arts in liberal arts in African and African American studies from Louisiana State University (LSU) in 2006. She later obtained a PhD in geography and anthropology from LSU in 2017. Her dissertation, "Producing 'Fabulous': Commodification and Ethnicity in Hair Braiding Salons," examines the expression and consumption of Africanness and femininity in hair salons in Baton Rouge, Louisiana, and Queens, New York. Greensword has also conducted ethnographic research in Jamaica (Ocho Rios, Kingston, and Kitson Town) that focused on how beauty is consumed and produced in hair braiding salons. Greensword has also taught college readiness, sociology, psychology, French, and Spanish at the secondary level for 14 years. Pres-

About the Contributors • **137**

ently, she is an adjunct instructor and postdoctoral fellow at Texas Christian University's Race and Reconciliation Initiative.

Sandra Hannigan (BA, MAT) is an instructional technologist at Northampton Community College (NCC), and adjunct instructor in the School of STEM teaching introduction to information technology. She earned a BA in education from New Jersey City University and an MAT from Webster University in Kansas City, MO specializing in technology in the classroom. Additionally, she taught junior high students in New Jersey, Kansas, and Missouri, became a global training manager and instructional designer at Gateway Computers, Inc., and an adjunct instructor at two community colleges in the Midwest. Her skills include instructional design, curriculum design, training and development facilitation, using technology in the classroom and presenting at higher education conferences. Along with her colleague, Lealan Zaccone, she co-developed a 101-onboarding course for new online instructors at NCC. She currently resides in Easton, PA.

Erica Heflin-Queen, EdD, earned her doctorate in educational leadership from The George Washington University. She is an educator with over 22 years of experience as a reading specialist in Maryland schools. Her work has been centered around providing reading intervention, helping teachers become great teachers of reading, working with school-based reading specialists and principals in the implementation of reading curriculum across the district, and boosting the culture of literacy within schools and communities. Currently, Dr. Heflin-Queen serves as an assistant principal. Dr. Heflin-Queen teaches as adjunct faculty for several community colleges in Maryland, including Harford Community College and Anne Arundel Community College, where she teaches developmental reading and writing as well as reading education courses for preservice teachers.

Sabrina F. Hinton, EdD, is a native of Winston-Salem, NC, and proud alumnae of Winston-Salem State University, Salem College, and Grand Canyon University. Hinton advocates for equity and equality in the early childhood education sector. Currently, Dr. Hinton serves as a professor and university supervisor in the Department of Education at Winston-Salem State University. Beyond her work in higher education, she owns and operates a network of early learning centers in the Winston-Salem/Forsyth County area, specializing in providing affordable, high-quality childcare and early education to the community. Further, Dr. Hinton utilizes her spare time to advocate for young children by donating time to community organizations like Smart Start of Forsyth County, Leadership Winston-Salem, and various educator networks. Dr. Hinton is the author of the children's book "My Silence, My Voice," and she is committed to cultivating a vibrant and engaged community bringing awareness that will impact the world.

138 ▪ About the Contributors

Danny E. Malone Jr., PhD, is in his first year as an assistant professor of criminology at Coastal Carolina University. Dr. Malone teaches sociology and criminology courses, will help develop the new approved criminal justice major, and become an active member of the CCU community. His previous position was at Coker University as an assistant professor of sociology and criminology where in 6 years he earned tenure and promotion to associate professor. Dr. Malone also served as sociology program coordinator, criminal and social justice policy graduate coordinator, and African American studies specialization coordinator. His areas of expertise include demography, race/class/gender and criminology. Dr. Malone's teaching mantra comes from Dr. W. E. B Du Bois: "Education must not simply teach work—it must teach life." He enjoys engaging and challenging his students to reach their fullest potential and embraces the teacher–scholar model fully with publications in noted peer-reviewed journals.

Ramycia McGhee, EdD, is a Chicago native. She is a tenured professor of English and literature at Linn-Benton Community College. She serves on the Oregon Humanities board of directors. She is a member of Oregon State University's advisory board for the adult and higher education master's and doctoral programs, in addition, she is a board member of the League of Oregon Cities Women's Caucus. Moreover, Dr. McGhee is a contributing author to the book entitled *Teaching Beautiful Brilliant Black Girls*. She is a member of Alpha Kappa Alpha Sorority Incorporated and is the founder of the Valencia Cooper Second Chance Scholarship Opportunity Award which solely benefits Black/African American students who are or want to attend a community college in the state of Oregon. Dr. McGhee was just elected as the first Black woman to sit on the Albany City Council. In her spare time, she enjoys traveling, reading, dancing, and spending time with her friends, family, and her Shih Tzu Cupcake and collecting Black Barbies.

Sierra JêCre McKissick is a behavioral and spiritual health specialist and development coach committed to transforming lives through practical education. As a facilitator and development coach, she helps executives, small teams, and learning organizations develop creative strategies to improve the health and wellness of their staff and community. Sierra is also the founder of McKissick Health and Wellness, a digital education company that houses a growing brand portfolio that includes *One Choice Magazine*, The Experience, Help+ Membership, and SFM Design Studio.

Senemeht Olatunji serves as regional impact manager at myFutureNC, serving the Southwest and Piedmont-Triad regions of the state. Senemeht has over 17 combined years of instructional, administrative/leadership, and social work experience. This includes 6 years of experience working as a secondary educator and instructional coach and practice experience in

About the Contributors • **139**

mental health treatment, domestic violence and sexual assault, transitional housing and homelessness, and child welfare. Senemeht Olatunji most recently served as the director of the First Star College of Staten Island (CSI) Academy, in the college's Division of Student Affairs and Alumni Engagement. The academy provides a 4-year, college preparatory program to youth associated with the foster care system from the NY metro area. Senemeht is also adjunct faculty at the Silberman School of Social Work at Hunter College where she teaches Introduction to Social Work, Social Welfare Policy and Child Welfare Policy. Senemeht holds a Master of Social Work from Howard University and Bachelor of Arts in English from Marymount Manhattan College, and is a licensed clinical social worker.

Denise Portis, PhD, has worked as a psychology and gender and sexuality studies adjunct for 11 years in Anne Arundel and Baltimore County, Maryland. Dr. Portis has numerous disabilities that include late-deafened, balance, and mobility. Finn, a Golden Retriever, is her 3rd service dog partner. She has been blogging about disAbility for over 20 years at Hearing Elmo. Dr. Portis has been an active member of the Commission on Disability Issues committee in Anne Arundel County since 2012 and an active mentor for the APA. Dr. Portis has been awarded the John & Suanne Roueche Excellence Award, League for Innovation, and Equity & Inclusion Champion Award from Anne Arundel Community College. Her life journey quote comes from Helen Keller: "I am only one, but still, I am one. I cannot do everything, but still, I can do something; and because I cannot do everything, I will not refuse to do something that I can do."

Loubert "Lou" Senatus is the CEO of Forward Thought Movement, Inc. and the executive coach for SELAH V Coaching and has been a consummate advocate for the well-being of children, families, and communities across Miami Dade County. Lou has been involved with nonprofit organizations since he graduated from the University of Florida in 2007. He is a certified member of Phi Theta Kappa Leadership (PTK) studies since 2014 and serves as an adjunct faculty at Miami Dade College. Lou also serves on the executive board committee with his home chapter of Omega Psi Phi Fraternity, Inc., where he serves as co-chair of the scholarship committee. Lou is a certified life coach through the Certified Life Coaching Institute & Academy for Leadership Coaching and NLP. Lou hails from Little Haiti (in Miami), Florida, and is poised to complete his doctorate in community college leadership from Morgan State University in Fall 2022.

Shelagh Smith currently teaches writing at Mass Maritime Academy and Bridgewater State University. She has taught previously at a small liberal arts college on the South Shore, as well as the University of Massachusetts Dartmouth. In addition to her work teaching first-year composition, she has

140 · About the Contributors

taught technical and business writing courses, literature, and creative writing. Before embarking on a teaching career, she worked in the private industry as vice president of Search for a boutique executive search firm, placing candidates at all levels across a vast array of industries. She is the winner of the PEN New England Susan P. Bloom Discovery award and holds a master's degree in professional writing from the University of Massachusetts.

Karen Wagner-Clarke, EdD, is the senior research specialist at Kaizen Human Capital and an adjunct faculty member at Wilmington University, College of Business. Over her tenure, she has facilitated courses in four disciplines: organizational management, business management, human resource management, and economics. Dr. Wagner-Clarke holds exemplar-level instructor status at Wilmington University, demonstrating her engagement as a higher-education instructor and one that cares deeply about student success. In addition, she is skilled in writing and editing and regularly writes articles for Kaizen Human Capital and QuestionPro's *Experience Journal.* Dr. Wagner-Clarke received a Doctor of Education in organizational leadership, learning, and innovation from Wilmington University (EdD), a master's in professional human resources (MPHR) from Georgetown University, a master's in organizational leadership w/track in human resource management (MSOL) from Quinnipiac University, and a Bachelor of Science in business administration from Post University. Additionally, Dr. Wagner-Clarke is a SHRM senior Certified professional (SHRM-SCP).

Lealan Zaccone (BA, MS, MDE) is an adjunct professor at Northampton Community College (NCC) and lead psychology instructor at Washington and Thornton Academy for International students from all over the world. Lealan has worked in higher education administration for over 20 years, specializing in the community college environment, and providing teaching and learning support of online education. Her educational background is in online pedagogy, education and training, and clinical psychology. She earned a BA degree from Moravian University, studied counseling psychology at Loyola College and received a master's in distance education from the University of Maryland Global Campus including several certificates in online teaching. Along with her colleague, Sandra Hannigan, she codesigned and facilitated an onboarding DIST 101 adjunct teaching orientation for all new online instructors at NCC. She currently resides in Bethlehem, Pennsylvania and enjoys traveling the world any chance she gets.

Printed in the United States
by Baker & Taylor Publisher Services